Brick Walls

Brick Walls

Reflections on Race in a Southern School District

Thomas E. Truitt

UNIVERSITY OF SOUTH CAROLINA PRESS

© 2006 University of South Carolina

Published by the University of South Carolina Press
Columbia, South Carolina 29208

www.sc.edu/uscpress

Manufactured in the United States of America

15 14 13 12 11 10 09 08 07 06   10 9 8 7 6 5 4 3 2 1

Library of Congress Cataloging-in-Publication Data

Truitt, Thomas E., 1940–
    Brick walls : reflections on race in a southern school district / Thomas E. Truitt.
        p. cm.
    Includes index.
    ISBN-13: 978-1-57003-638-5 (cloth : alk. paper)
    ISBN-10: 1-57003-638-1 (cloth : alk. paper)
    1. School integration—South Carolina—Florence—History—20th century.
2. African American children—Education—South Carolina—Florence—History—
20th century. 3. Florence Public Schools (S.C.). District One. 4. Florence (S.C.)—
Race relations. I. Title.
    LC214.23.F56T78 2006
    371.829'960757—dc22

                                                                    2006005090

This book was printed on Glatfelter Natures Natural, a recycled paper with
50 percent post-consumer waste content.

Contents

Preface vii

Acknowledgments ix

Part I

1 A Shameful History 3

2 Integration Lite 6

3 Lawsuits 9

4 Inching Forward 12

Part II

5 A New School 17

6 Welcome to Florence 19

7 Into the Frying Pan 21

8 Name Calling 25

9 Palace Coup 29

10 Pouring Gasoline on the Fires 33

11 Campaigning 38

12 Where Do You Put a School? 41

13 A Whitewashed Election 47

14 Searching for a Site 52

15 Flawed Firing 55

16 Public Meetings 58

17 Working with Justice 65

18 North Vista Education Plan 70

19 Board Decision 79

20 The Long, Hot Summer 87

21 Implementing the Plan 94

22 Justice Department Hearing 100

23 Teacher Dismissal 105

24 Running the Gauntlet 111

25 What Are You Going to Do
with Carver? 115

26 Single-Member District Hearing 122

27 Bailing Out 125

28 Changing Board Elections 128

29 A New Regime 134

30 Attorneys' Fees 141

31 Superintendent Search 144

Epilogue 154

Appendix: *Florence School
District One Board of Trustees* 159

Index 161

About the Author 165

Preface

Like a river dumping sediment downstream and cutting new channels, the past is a continuous, powerful current, shaping people and events, altering the future. We can no more disconnect the past from present and future events than we can take a part of a river, lift it from its channel, and move it to a new location. The past, present, and future are continuous and connected.

Nowhere is the past more significant than in the "history haunted" South. To talk about any event in the South without some analysis of history is as precarious as driving on a six-lane highway without an occasional glance in the rearview mirror.

Looking back to 1954, we see the *Brown v. Board of Education* decision by the U.S. Supreme Court declaring separation of the races in schools unconstitutional. NAACP lawyer, and later U.S. Supreme Court justice, Thurgood Marshall thought the schools would be integrated within five years, but even after fifty years of struggle, schools in the South and other parts of the country are not integrated.

When I came to Florence, South Carolina, in 1987 to become superintendent of schools, the district had one all-black school and five others that were racially identifiable.* Even though the *Brown* decision had been announced over forty years earlier, Florence had not adopted an integration plan for its schools.

This is the story of how Florence achieved a court-ordered plan for integrating its schools. It is a story of conflicts between the races played out in the school district, and it is the story of the building of Carver Elementary School, the key event that led to student attendance zones and school board elections being turned upside down.

---

* A racially identifiable school, as defined by the U.S. Department of Justice, is one in which the racial percentages of the student body vary more than 15 percent from the averages for the district as a whole.

This story cannot be understood in isolation. To understand what happened in Florence School District One in the 1990s and the problems with building a replacement Carver Elementary School, one has to look first at how the Florence community and the state of South Carolina has educated its children over the years. This is part 1 of the book.

Part 2 is a personal account of the building of Carver Elementary School and the events pressing in on, and emanating from, that process as told by the superintendent who was responsible for building the school.

If you go by Carver Elementary School on Cashua Drive today, you will see a beautiful school sitting well back from the road. If you come up the winding drive and enter the building, you will be greeted by soft classical music at the door. If you wander around, you will see a colorful, clean building populated by happy children and hard-working teachers and staff, but you will not know anything about the struggle to build the school and how that struggle changed the Florence School District One and the Florence community.

For that story, read on.

Acknowledgments

I am grateful to each Florence School District Number One trustee who served on the school board during my eleven years as superintendent in that district. Board member service, particularly in times of high conflict, is a taxing and stressful experience. I appreciate the willingness of board members to contribute their talents and energy to this community service.

A list of these board members may be found in the appendix. I am indebted to them for allowing me to serve Florence School District One for eleven years as its superintendent.

People care deeply about their children and their schools, but since they do not always agree on what is best, there will be conflict. In a school district, much of this conflict focuses on the school board and superintendent. A superintendent works for the board, not individual board members, and must follow the direction of the majority of the board. This sometimes puts a superintendent in conflict with board members who hold minority views.

Because the conflict described in this story is written from a participant's point of view, some persons may be viewed as antagonists. This is a function of the structure of the book and is intended to describe the dramatic tension that occurs when there are divergent opinions and beliefs. There is no intent to demean or besmirch the character or integrity of persons who were on opposite sides of the conflicts described in this book.

This is a true story, a recent history. Real names are used in this book with the few exceptions noted in the footnotes.

Although true, the book is written as creative nonfiction, a genre that uses many devices normally associated with fiction, such as dialogue, to tell a story. The reader will find such dialogues throughout the book.

Some journalists worry about the increasingly blurred line between fiction and nonfiction, but most agree that quotes can be used as long as they are not invented and they represent—as accurately as memory allows—the truth.

None of the quotes in the book are invented. I was present when the statements were made and kept notes and a journal, transcribing as accurately as I could what was said in meetings and conferences. These quotes are based on my journal and represent what I believe was said. There is no intent to deceive or embellish.

This book had its beginnings in 1996, in the midst of the conflict over the building of Carver Elementary School, when I was faced with the requirement to renew my superintendent's certificate. I called Dr. Robert Parham, head of the English department at Francis Marion University, and told him I wanted to take a writing course. Uneasy about taking a formal course, I asked Dr. Parham about an independent study, hoping to work privately with a professor. Dr. Parham would not agree to this request and recommended I take advanced composition under Dr. Ken Autrey.

Each Tuesday night for a semester, I, a fifty-six-year-old school superintendent, sat in class with twenty juniors and seniors at Francis Marion University and learned from a master teacher. Although I was uncomfortable at first, Ken made me feel welcome and comfortable, and he helped me grow as a writer. My final project in his class became a chapter is this book. I am indebted to Ken for encouraging me to write this book.

Three online writer friends deserve thanks for reading and critiquing my manuscript. At a time when I was about to give up on the book, Cherie Kuranko of Orting, Washington, offered to critique it for me. Encouraged by her suggestions, I continued to revise the book.

Subsequently, Dena Harris of Greensboro, North Carolina, and Betsy O'Brien Harrison of Pittsburgh, Pennsylvania, read the manuscript and offered many useful suggestions and encouragement.

I also owe a special debt to my sister, Susan Schindler of Philadelphia, a senior editor for Merck, who read the book and helped get it in proper form.

Special thanks also go to Dr. Sandra Tonnsen, formerly of the University of South Carolina and currently professor of education at Western Carolina University, who provided helpful feedback on the book.

I will always be grateful to Alexander Moore, acquisitions editor at the University of South Carolina, who had faith in me and this book and who stuck with me during the many months it took to bring it to publication.

Part I

A Shameful
ONE **History**

South Carolina's education record is dismal. Before the Civil War, South Carolina law proscribed the education of slaves. This situation changed briefly in 1868 when a group of African Americans, northerners, and "scalawag" white natives met in Charleston to rewrite the state's constitution. The 1868 document guaranteed free public schools for all children.

After Reconstruction, with white native South Carolinians again in control, the new state government cut spending for schools and instituted policies that widened the gap between white and black schools. In 1880 white schools received an average of $2.75 per pupil, while black schools received $2.51. By 1895 the state was spending $3.11 per white student and had reduced spending on black students to $1.05 per pupil.*

In 1895, when the state adopted a new constitution, segregated schools were mandated by the following clause: "Separate schools shall be provided for children of the white and colored races, and no child of either race shall ever be permitted to attend a school provided for children of the other race."

But segregation could not stand against the growing demands for justice that began in 1948 when Levi Pearson, an African American farmer in Clarendon County, made the first move to chip away at the wall separating schoolchildren of South Carolina by race. Pearson filed a lawsuit against the Clarendon County School Board asking it to provide funds to operate a bus.

When he filed the lawsuit, Pearson wasn't trying to improve the state's education system for African Americans. He was unaware that 62 percent of the adult black population was either totally or functionally illiterate.† He just wanted the

---

* Virginia Ward, ed., "The History of South Carolina Schools: A Tragic Tale," study commissioned and published online by the South Carolina Center for Teacher Recruitment, Retention, and Advancement, http://www.sccerra.org (accessed June 9, 2005).

† Walter Edgar, *South Carolina in the Modern Age* (Columbia: University of South Carolina Press, 1992), 99.

school board to buy some gas for the rickety, old school bus he and other black parents had purchased so their children wouldn't have to walk to school. At the time Clarendon County operated thirty buses for white children but none for African Americans, although they outnumbered white children three to one in the system.

Although Pearson's suit was thrown out of court, the black citizens were not deterred. They connected with Columbia attorney Harold Boulware, who secured help from Thurgood Marshall, a young attorney for the National Association for the Advancement of Colored People (NAACP).

The group filed a new suit, *Briggs v. Elliott*, initially seeking equal facilities for their children, later challenging segregated schools. When they lost again, this time in federal court in Charleston, they appealed to the United States Supreme Court.

Briggs was consolidated with four other desegregation cases making their way through the federal court system and came to the U.S. Supreme Court as part of *Brown v. Board of Education of Topeka*. On May 17, 1954, by a unanimous vote, the U.S. Supreme Court justices ruled that schools segregated by race are unconstitutional.

Even before the *Brown* decision, the state of South Carolina had dug in its heels. Anticipating pressure to desegregate, in 1952 the legislature authorized a referendum to delete the constitutional provision requiring the state to maintain public schools. The referendum passed overwhelmingly.* South Carolinians preferred to close their schools rather than integrate them. Schools remained opened in South Carolina, but private schools flourished.

In *Brown* the U.S. Supreme Court had decreed schools be desegregated "with all deliberate speed." In South Carolina deliberation took precedence over speed. Nine years passed before any African American students attended school with whites. In 1963, 11 black students in Charleston were the first to attend formerly all-white schools. The following year 266 African American students attended previously all-white schools. In 1965–66 the number had grown to 3,200.

Like many South Carolina districts, Florence School District One adopted a "freedom-of-choice" plan that allowed black students to attend previously all-white schools. In the 1964–65 school year, the first black students attended previously all-white McClenaghan High School. The following year 89 blacks attended seven previously all-white schools.

Under the cumbersome freedom-of-choice procedures that required parents to choose schools each spring, school integration inched forward. In July 1967 a delegation of the Florence NAACP asked the school board what was being done to integrate the schools.

* Edgar, *South Carolina in the Modern Age*, 100.

According to the Florence One Board minutes, the superintendent, Henry Sneed, told the group that 460 "Negro children" had attended previously all-white schools that year. Sneed added that four "Negro teachers" were teaching in white schools and seven or eight white teachers were working in "Negro schools."

Although slow to integrate, Florence moved more quickly than most of the state. In 1969 Florence School District One was one of twelve of the state's ninety-three districts that had admitted black students to previously all-white schools.

Integration moved forward gradually in Florence, but it did so without violent disruptions in the schools. Not all South Carolina communities were as fortunate.

The most violent event in the desegregation struggle took place in Orangeburg. On February 6, 1968, students from South Carolina State College tried to integrate the All Star Bowling Lane in Orangeburg. The owner refused. Two days later two hundred students gathered around a bonfire built on a campus street. When policemen smothered the bonfire, students retaliated by throwing rocks and bottles at the lawmen.

After the policemen left, the students built another bonfire. When the lawmen returned to put out the second fire, someone hit one of them with a banister post and more rocks were thrown. The policemen opened fire.

When the smoke cleared, twenty-seven students had been shot; three, fatally. The nine patrolmen charged with the shootings were all acquitted. The event became known as the "Orangeburg Massacre."

Not until 2001, when then Governor Jim Hodges expressed regret over it, did the state show any remorse for the incident. In 2003 Governor Mark Sanford apologized for the shootings.

TWO **Integration Lite**

In 1960 when Florentines spoke of the "other side of the tracks," the term had a literal racial meaning. First settled as a railroad town, the growing community was split by two railroad tracks—one ran north to south, one east to west. No blacks lived south of the east/west railroad, and few whites lived east of the north/south line.

That year, having just completed twelve months in a federal court clerkship, Laurence McIntosh came to town to practice law. Fascinated by the evolving case law of school desegregation suits, the young lawyer read extensively on the subject and became recognized as the local expert on the topic, frequently speaking at local civic clubs.

In 1970 the federal government brought suits against all school districts in South Carolina, demanding they desegregate their schools. Since his law firm represented Florence School District One, McIntosh was the logical choice to defend the district in its desegregation suit.

While Florence and most South Carolina districts were under pressure to desegregate, Greenville and Darlington were singled out for special attention. Fed up with the resistance to integration, in January 1970 the South Carolina NAACP asked the courts to order immediate desegregation of these two districts. The court sided with the NAACP and ordered the districts to integrate fully and immediately. On February 16, 1970, the Greenville and Darlington schools opened with total integration.

For several weeks three thousand white students in Darlington County (adjacent to Florence) boycotted their schools. On March 3, 1970, a mob of one hundred fifty white adults, men and women, overturned a school bus in Lamar, a small Darlington community. Twenty-two of the protestors were indicted, and eighteen were found guilty. Three men requested and received jury trials. An all-white jury found them guilty of common law rioting and assault and battery of a high nature. Each received a jail sentence and a fine.

By summer 1970 McIntosh had become engaged to be married. He remembers having to leave early from a party for his bride-to-be and him to make the long drive to Spartanburg to defend the school district before federal judge Donald Russell.

Both the Justice Department and the Florence school district presented plans to Judge Russell. While the school district's plan was lacking in many ways, the federal plan was unworkable.

The federal plan created long corridors, cutting across the community, carving out bizarre school zones. In addition to the gerrymandered zones, the Justice Department plan was seriously flawed, assigning students beyond the capacities of several schools.

Judge Russell gave the Justice Department sixty days to present a workable plan. When it failed to meet the deadline, the Florence school district opened the 1970–71 school year under its original plan.

The politically savvy McIntosh worked with Senator Strom Thurmond's office to gain approval of the Florence plan, trading on Richard Nixon's debt to the South Carolina senator. In 1964 Thurmond had switched from the Democratic to the Republican Party and had been a vital cog in the 1968 southern strategy that propelled Nixon into the White House.

Additionally, in his campaigning for the presidency, Nixon had represented himself as an opponent of busing. Under his administration the Justice Department quit pushing integration, and Florence was left to implement its integration plan without federal supervision.

The initial integration of the Florence school system was overseen by an all-white school board, elected under a system that made it impossible for blacks to win a seat on the board. Board members were elected annually at a meeting held at the McClenaghan High School, an all-white school. With few blacks attending the meetings, none was elected.

In the late sixties, with pressure mounting to put an African American on the board, Laurence McIntosh, as board attorney, devised a plan to have an African American take a board seat.

Having reached an understanding with the legislative delegation to appoint a black, McIntosh arranged for Dr. Julian Price, a respected white pediatrician and long-term board member, to resign in the middle of his term. The delegation appointed Theodore Lester, the first black member of the board.

In March 1970 Lester faced his first election at the annual citizens' meeting. Normally a few dozen people attended the meeting, but a proposal to increase school taxes by sixteen mills, partly to make improvements in the black schools, drew a huge crowd. The location was moved from the auditorium to the gymnasium, but still the crowd overflowed the room.

The tax increase was defeated 3,136 to 943, but Lester was elected to the board, the last time board members were elected at the annual meeting.

Because the citizens' meeting had grown unmanageable, the Florence County legislative delegation changed the method of selecting board members, setting up a nine-member board with members, elected at-large, serving three-year terms. Since the new system provided for run-off elections when candidates did not receive a majority of the votes, blacks still had difficulty being elected. Theodore Lester remained the lone black member of the board.

Even though now represented on the board, the black community was impatient with the pace of progress, becoming less accepting of tokenism. The change in tone from asking to demanding is illustrated by the appearance of Frank Gilbert before the Florence School District One Board on September 13, 1973.

Gilbert, a black counselor at Wilson High School, had been appointed to the Florence County Board of Education and was having trouble obtaining permission from the Florence One Board to get thirty minutes off to attend the meetings.

Gilbert told the board, "I do not seek your love necessarily, but I demand your respect. If you desire coexistence, let us walk and live together like men. If you desire extinction, let us fight by whatever means available."

The next fight would be over the location of a new Wilson High School.

THREE **Lawsuits**

Located in the heart of the African American community on Irby Street in the building now occupied by the Bethel Apostolic Church, Wilson High School had 696 black students and 59 white students in 1970. Until 1970 the school had served an all-black population.

In an effort to attract more white students to the school, the board decided to replace Wilson with a new facility and purchased a parcel of land on Highway 327 about five miles from the existing school. Controversy swirled around the decision to move the school, and on April 20, 1976, the board held a public hearing at Wilson High School to receive comments about the proposed location.

In a practice that seems odd even for that time, the board minutes identified speakers by race. Each white speaker had a "w" after his name, and each black speaker had a "b."

Of the thirteen white speakers at the hearing, eight advocated moving the school to the proposed location; two favored renovating at the present site; and three expressed no preference.

No black speaker favored moving to the proposed location. Twelve speakers urged the board to renovate at the present site or acquire property in the black neighborhood, while two expressed no preference for location.

Rev. W. P. Diggs summarized the position of the black speakers when he said, "The black man has been deprived over and over again. . . . Acquire property in the community and build a new school in this community."

Freddie Jolley, a young African American who had recently come to Florence, also spoke at the hearing. Two years before coming to Florence, Jolley had served as a fellow for the Ford Foundation, spending time with the Department of Health, Education, and Welfare and the Lawyers Committee for Civil Rights in Washington, D.C.; the Southeastern Regional Council in Atlanta; and the Columbia Urban League in Columbia, South Carolina. Employed by the American

Friends Service Committee as an advocate for students, Jolley was trained and prepared to be a community activist.

In his remarks at the hearing, Jolley chastised the school board, saying, "The only reason you want to move this school is because of its black heritage."

But Jolley was more than fiery rhetoric. After the hearing, drawing on his experience as a community activist, he invoked a little known opportunity to object and filed a complaint with the Environmental Protection Agency (EPA), insisting a study of the proposed site be done before the school was built. Such a study would not only delay the school's construction but would be expensive for the school board.

Superintendent Bruce Crowley and the board's chair, George Jordan, met privately with Jolley and urged him to withdraw his complaint. Although he had spoken out against moving the school, Jolley understood the need to attract more whites to Wilson and opposed the proposed site only because it was too far from town. He asked Crowley and Jordan to find another site.

Within months the school board had located a site on the Old Marion Highway, closer to the black community but in a more "neutral" spot. Jolley withdrew his complaint, and the school was built.

A year later Jolley ran for the school board, collecting over 5,700 votes but losing by thirteen votes to a white female Francis Marion College professor. Jolley was not alone in his failure to win a school board seat. Other black candidates were meeting the same fate. Blacks still held only one seat on the nine-member board.

Although school board elections were at-large (meaning registered voters throughout the district could vote for any candidate), seats were numbered. With no residential requirements attached to the seats, candidates could declare for the seat of their choice.

Exercising this choice, candidates tried to gain political advantage. Any time a black ran for a board seat, a white could declare for that same seat. Given the voting pattern of the community, the white was virtually assured of winning.

After being reelected in 1970, Theodore Lester resigned in 1973 over concerns about the board's unresponsiveness to the black community and for health reasons. Calvin Thomas became the second African American to serve on the board when he was appointed to replace Lester.

When appointed to the board, Thomas was a twenty-something parent with one child in school and another about to begin. The Florence NAACP opposed the appointment of Thomas, viewing him as the white community's candidate because of his relationship with Laurence Hill, a white board member. Hill had noticed Thomas's involvement in the Greenwood PTA and thought the young man would make a good board member. After his appointment, Thomas worked hard to convince local NAACP leaders that he would be an effective representative for them. Thomas later became president of the group's local chapter.

Thomas was unopposed in 1976 and was reelected to the board, remaining the lone African American on the school board.

In June 1978 Freddie Jolley, Eugene Pierce, Leonye Cunningham, John Jones, Madie Robinson, and W. P. Diggs filed suit against the Florence School District One Board, citing the underrepresentation of blacks on the board. The case never went to court, and over the next three years the attorneys negotiated, looking for a solution acceptable to both sides.

In February 1981 the board's attorney, Laurence McIntosh, recommended the board modify the system of electing members by dropping the numbered seats and the requirement to win a majority of the votes. Additionally, one-shot voting would now be permitted. Previously, voters were required to vote for three candidates. When fewer than three black candidates ran, blacks were required to vote for whites. The single-shot method, which allowed voters to vote for one, two, or three candidates in the school board election, allowed blacks to advance the cause of their candidates without also voting for whites.

After a forty-minute discussion, the board voted (7–2) to accept the change. The plaintiffs dropped their complaint, and the new system was adopted. Henceforth candidates in school board elections would run at-large, without having to declare for a specific seat. There would be no runoffs. The top three vote getters would gain seats on the board.

FOUR Inching Forward

For years the black citizens of Florence had lobbied, unsuccessfully, to have an African American appointed to one of the assistant superintendent positions. When the assistant superintendent for instruction, Joe Bonds, resigned in 1980 to become superintendent in Fort Mill, South Carolina, Florence superintendent Crowley decided to recruit an African American to fill the position.

Dr. Joe Heyward had a track record with the district, having been a teacher, assistant principal, and principal. In 1973, while serving as principal of Williams Middle School, Heyward resigned to take a position with Francis Marion College. Seven years later Crowley invited Heyward to come back to the district as assistant superintendent for instruction.

The board, with only one black member, was not as eager as Crowley to place an African American in the upper levels of the school administration. When Crowley first presented Heyward's name to the board, some members balked. Some were bothered that Heyward had not applied for the job. Others wondered if he had been out of public education too long. Some wanted the position to go to a white, female administrator in the district who made no bones about her interest in, and qualifications for, the job.

To smooth the way for Heyward's appointment, Crowley, the board chair, Belva High, and the district personnel director, John Danner, met with Heyward. After this meeting the board approved Heyward for the position by an 8–1 vote.

A month later Frank Gilbert appeared before the board to commend them on the hiring of Joe Heyward as assistant superintendent for instruction. Gilbert called the board's action timely and courageous. Noting that blacks had always been discriminated against, Gilbert praised the board for hiring a black assistant superintendent.

There's no evidence that Crowley's push to hire a black assistant superintendent caused him problems with the board, but he was out less than a year later. He submitted his resignation in January 1981, which the board accepted 5–4.

In spring 1981 board elections, Freddie Jolley was once again a candidate and was again unsuccessful. But James Byrd, who owned the Curtis Mathes television franchise in Florence, was elected. Byrd, along with Calvin Thomas, gave the black community two members on the board. Two years later, with the election of Maggie Glover, the board had three African Americans serving simultaneously.

From the seventy-three candidates who applied to replace Crowley, the board chose Jim Womack, a New Yorker with a master's degree from Harvard. A short, intense, energetic man, Womack launched the district into an ambitious accountability system called the Standards. Ahead of his time, Womack devoted district resources to developing tests for each subject for each grade to measure student process. For his efforts, he was named to the *Executive Educator*'s list of the 100 Best School Administrators in the nation. He also alienated teachers who feared the Standards would be used to implement merit pay or fire teachers.

After two years of working with Womack, Joe Heyward returned to Francis Marion College. When Womack replaced Heyward with Jack Sullivan, the white principal of West Florence High School, the district was again without a black assistant superintendent; and the black community again began pushing for change in the district.

Two months after Heyward's return to higher education, Madie Robinson of the NAACP addressed the board about the lack of blacks in leadership positions.

In his normal style of meeting problems head-on, Womack met with representatives of the NAACP. After a series of meetings with these representatives, Womack created a new position—district recruiter—and, in December 1984, hired Patricia Davis, an African American who taught English at South Florence High School.

Not only did the hiring of Davis bring another African American into the district office administration, it facilitated connections with historically black colleges. Womack charged Davis with increasing the number of black teachers in the district.

But Davis could not change the complexion of the district teaching staff overnight. The issue of insufficient numbers of black teachers continued to dog the board.

On July 1, 1985, Womack received a letter from David Lucas, NAACP president, and Joe Heyward, the chair of the NAACP Education Committee. The letter raised several concerns, including hiring practices, lack of black administrators, the absence of contracts with minority businesses, the disposition of the old Wilson High School building, and salaries for substitute teachers.

Womack responded by appointing district staff to work with the NAACP on ways to address the concerns.

Although the South Carolina School Boards Association named him Superintendent of the Year, Womack made enemies in the community. He expected board members to follow his recommendations and reacted badly when they did not. Womack also alienated business leaders with his hard push to raise the millage rates.

In December 1986 a teacher at West Florence High School lost her patience with a defiant student and used the "N" word. Incensed, the African American community demanded the teacher be fired. Womack suspended the teacher for three days and wrote a letter of reprimand saying any future lapses of judgment would result in dismissal.

In a school district that required voter approval to raise taxes, Womack had alienated too many people in the community, reducing the possibility of gaining voter approval for tax increases. In February 1987 the board voted not to extend his contract. Rather than remain as a lame duck, Womack negotiated a buyout of his contract and left the district.

Joe Heyward described Womack as "different," unable to adjust to the community. Ten years after he left Florence, district office personnel were still telling stories about Womack. The one that defined the highly organized and demanding Womack was the tale of how his daily wear was selected. Each day Womack required his wife to lay out two outfits for him. After he chose one, she had to put the other back and repeat the process the next day.

In May, and again in June, the board asked the voters to approve an increase in taxes for school operation. The voters rejected both requests, forcing the board to use $1.3 million from its reserve fund for the 1987–88 school year. Without an increase in taxes, the district would be bankrupt by the end of 1988.

In late spring 1987, the board went looking for a new superintendent.

Part II

FIVE A New School

I sang along with my radio, patting my hand on the steering wheel, keeping time with the music. Florence voters had just approved a $14.3 million bond referendum. For the first time in my seventeen years as a superintendent, I would be involved in building new schools.

It was September 22, 1992, the day after the bond referendum, and I was on my way to Carver Elementary School to celebrate with Principal Dorothy Ellerbe.

Nearly fifty years old, Carver School consisted of two buildings and six mobile classrooms, squeezed onto a six-acre plot of low land. After a good rain, the playground looked like a fishpond.

As with many schools built for African Americans during segregation, the school board had skimped on construction costs and neglected the building's maintenance over the years. Water seeped into classrooms from the ground, puddling on the linoleum floors. The roof leaked. Ceiling tiles were stained and, from time to time, crashed down on the vulnerable students and teachers. Mold and mildew flourished throughout the building. Paint peeled off the walls. With outdated, inadequate lighting, the building was dark, dreary, and depressing.

In spite of the deplorable conditions at Carver, the driving force behind the referendum was the desire to relieve crowded conditions at three predominantly white K–6 schools—Briggs, Royall, and Savannah Grove. These three schools, located in the southern and western sections of the district, attracted white growth. White students in each school were 65 percent or more of the total population, and their numbers were increasing. To accommodate the expanding student populations, the board had placed mobile units at these schools.

The usual solution to the problem of overcrowding is to build a new school and rezone to relieve the overcrowded ones. But rezoning Briggs, Royall, and Savannah Grove would be politically unpopular. No one wanted to leave these schools.

My staff and I came up with an alternative. We recommended building a new middle school to house grades 7 and 8 and relieving the overcrowding by removing grades 5 and 6 from the three elementary schools and putting them in the existing middle school serving the area. The plan solved the overcrowding in the three elementary schools without rezoning. Rather than serving grades K–6, these schools would now serve grades K–4. After fourth grade, students in these schools would have to change schools, but they would move in groups, staying together.

The board approved this plan and decided to build a new middle school. As an afterthought, they added a replacement school for Carver to the bond package, a political gambit to secure black votes for the bond referendum.

When I walked into the principal's office, Dorothy Ellerbe sprang to her feet and walked around her desk to greet me, her smile gleaming. She asked, "Dr. Truitt, do you really think we will get a new school? I bet they build the new middle school and never get around to Carver."

I said, "Dorothy, the new Carver School will be ready before the middle school. In fact, you may be in it a year before the middle school is built."

Although a school superintendent for seventeen years, I had never been involved in building a new school. Naively, with the funding in place and approved by 60 percent of the district voters, I thought it would be smooth sailing.

I was wrong.

Welcome to
SIX Florence

When the Florence School District One Board went looking for a superintendent in late spring 1987, I was completing my twelfth year as superintendent of the Danville Public Schools, in Virginia. My son had left home for college, and I was looking for a new challenge. When I saw the Florence advertisement for a superintendent, I applied. Then my wife, Judy, and I drove to Florence for a weekend. Finding the community attractive, Judy gave me her blessing to pursue the Florence job.

When I hadn't received a response to my application by early June, I thought we had wasted a trip to Florence. I was concerned about leaving Danville so near the opening of the school year, and I planned to withdraw my application if I didn't hear from Florence before a late-June trip I had planned to Charleston, South Carolina. Three days before I was to leave for Charleston, John Cone, who was executive director of the South Carolina School Boards Association (SCSBA) and was directing the search, called and asked me to come to Florence for an interview at the exact time I would be passing through on my way to Charleston.

In late June I met the nine-member board—seven white, two black; six men, three women—in the district office building. In round-robin fashion, they asked me a series of prepared questions. Although I didn't know the specifics of South Carolina law or financing, I felt good about my answers. After seventy-five minutes I was back on the road to Charleston.

A week later John Cone called and invited me for a second interview on July 5. This interview was held in the cafeteria of Florence General Hospital, and the board members didn't ask prepared questions. We talked informally throughout the dinner. I relaxed and gave candid answers to their questions. When the interview ended at 9:15, I jumped in my car and headed back to Danville.

Working for one boss is easy, but superintendents work for boards (in Florence, nine people). Even though a board is composed of different people, the group has a distinct personality and character. To succeed, a superintendent must be compatible with the board's personality. I knew I had connected with the Florence board at both interviews. On the way back to Danville, I stopped and called Judy. I told her, "I'm their man."

A week later Calvin Thomas, who now chaired the board, called to say I was their choice. On July 22, I drove 190 miles to Florence for a press conference and my introduction to the community. In less than four weeks, I would be on the job.

On my first day of work, August 17, 1987, a reporter from the *Florence Morning News* followed my every step. At noon I did a live television interview outside of Southside Middle School. In ninety-eight-degree temperatures, I struggled to speak coherently, fighting the temptation to swat the tenacious South Carolina gnats from my face.

I was unaware of Florence's history of racial divisiveness, but had I known, I would not have worried. Few forty-seven-year-olds had more experience in dealing with racial issues in schools than I brought to Florence. As a principal in the late sixties, I had integrated a junior high school in Burlington, North Carolina. In Danville I had been an assistant superintendent during the time of a school integration court case that was appealed to the U.S. Supreme Court, and I had helped devise and implement the integration plan for that system. In spite of this background, I was unprepared for the bitterness, suspicion, and mistrust I found in Florence.

Into the Frying Pan

A little over a month after school started, the first racial issue boiled up. An African American study-hall supervisor had made inappropriate remarks to female students at a middle school. The principal recommended that the man be dismissed.

The principal had begun her investigation based on one or two initial reports. As she probed further, she found other students to corroborate the original testimony. In considering the principal's recommendation, I noted that fourteen students had verified the supervisor's remarks, and I supported the recommendation to dismiss.

Florence School Board policies gave employees, such as the study-hall supervisor, the right to a hearing before the superintendent. If the superintendent supported the dismissal, the employee could appeal to the board. The involvement of the school board in the final decision to dismiss noncertificated employees was radically different from Danville's personnel procedures. In twelve years as superintendent in Danville, I had never dealt with the dismissal of a noncertificated employee. There an assistant superintendent handled all such actions; the board was never involved. But the Florence School Board was elected and liked to respond to constituents. Board members wanted the final say in the firing of all personnel.

The absence of the accusing students, who were African American, gave the hearing a racial overtone with the white principal and assistant superintendent for personnel recommending dismissal of an African American employee represented by an African American lawyer with three dozen African American supporters in attendance.

The study-hall supervisor asked to have the hearing open to the public so his supporters could hear the testimony. He claimed the students were getting back at him for disciplining them. Numerous supporters testified for the supervisor, proclaiming his good character. One witness, a man involved in local politics, made a thinly veiled threat against me, saying I would be sorry if I recommended the supervisor's dismissal.

I believed the evidence presented by the principal and concluded the man should be fired, but recognizing the tension in the situation, I called the board's attorney, Laurence McIntosh, for advice. I told Laurence about the hearing, expressing my surprise at the number of supporters who came on behalf of the study-hall supervisor.

"Tom, you're new here. You're off to a good start as superintendent, but you need the black community on your side. You don't want to get them against you so early in your tenure here. Why don't you find a compromise that will enable the man to keep his job?"

I considered Laurence's suggestion for about five seconds. With twelve years experience as a superintendent, I knew compromise was necessary at times, but in this case, I felt the supervisor was a threat to the well being of the students.

"Laurence, the man needs to be fired. I have to look out for the welfare of students. He doesn't need to be working around children. My biggest concern is how to proceed from here. I don't want to go through a three-hour hearing before the board."

"Let me make a suggestion. Let's get the board to hear the case 'on the record.'"

"How does that work?"

"It means that the board will review the hearing you've just held. They will hear no new testimony. The lawyers can be present and make brief statements, but there can be no new testimony."

Recognizing that this procedure would prevent a long, drawn-out hearing before the board, I said, "I like that. Let's do it."

A week later I wrote the supervisor and told him I was dismissing him. He appealed. Because of scheduling problems, the hearing before the board did not take place for several months. In the meantime another problem from Southside Middle School added to the developing racial tension. Two student witnesses said a fourteen-year-old African American eighth-grader had brought a gun to school. Although no gun was found, the principal recommended expulsion.

As I was leaving my office to go into the expulsion hearing, my secretary, Jerry Wilkes, her normally pale face flushed, burst in and said, "Freddie Jolley is out there."

"Who is Freddie Jolley?" I asked.

She told me Jolley was a community civil rights activist and a fervent and tenacious defender of black students in trouble.

When I entered the boardroom, I saw Jolley sitting beside the accused student. Jolley had a serious look on his face and a large Afro hairstyle.

The question of the gun dominated the hearing. Two witnesses said they saw it, but we had never recovered the gun. The board split on the issue: the majority believed the witnesses, but a minority did not want to expel the student without any tangible evidence. Weston Weldon, a former teacher of agriculture in the district, joined the African American board members, Calvin Thomas and Maggie Glover, in opposing the expulsion.

Lucy Davis, a former teacher, principal, and supervisor in the district, proposed a compromise, saying, "I agree this student should not go back to Southside Middle School, but what about letting him attend another school in the district?"

Carroll Player, a dentist serving his second term on the board, moved to put Lucy's idea into practice. He said, "I move we give the student the option of transferring to either Moore or Williams Middle School, contingent upon the acceptance of the school principal."

Carroll's motion passed, defusing the tension within the board over the student's fate by shifting the responsibility to two principals who were not at the hearing.*

A couple of weeks later the board, with seven members present, met to hear the case of the study-hall supervisor on the record. Once again the supervisor was represented by an attorney, but his supporters seemed to have lost interest, with only about ten in the audience.

After brief presentations by the supervisor's attorney and Laurence McIntosh, the board adjourned to executive session to consider the case in private. After an hour they returned and announced they had not reached a decision.

The next day I saw Lucy Davis at Briggs Elementary School and asked, "What happened?"

"We had four votes for dismissal, but three were for keeping him. I'm so mad with Calvin, Maggie, and Weston. I don't know what they were thinking. I got so mad that I just refused to vote. We'll have to vote the next time we meet."

I didn't understand Lucy's reluctance to vote on the night of the hearing, but a week later, at its first budget study of the year, the board, without discussion, voted for dismissal 4–3. The vote happened so quickly that Dick Frate, director of finance, was into his budget presentation before the supervisor's supporters knew it was over.

The next day I saw Calvin Thomas and, wanting to understand his position, asked him about his vote in the case. Calvin said, "It's not whether the supervisor was guilty or innocent. I felt like we should be consistent with what we have done in the past."

---

* Since neither of the other middle school principals agreed to accept the student, he was not allowed to return to school that year.

Calvin was referring to an incident that had taken place during Jim Womack's last year in Florence in which a black student had pushed a white teacher. In response, the teacher called the student a "nigger." Because that teacher had not been fired, Calvin thought it was wrong to fire the supervisor.

I saw differences in the two cases. In one, a teacher had called a student a name in reaction to being pushed. In the other, an employee displayed a pattern of making inappropriate comments to students, comments that appeared to be designed to insinuate himself into the students' sexual world.

The study-hall supervisor's dismissal hearing gave me my first lesson on racial attitudes in Florence, South Carolina. Lesson number two was fast on its heels.

EIGHT **Name Calling**

A week later I met with the South Florence High School girls' basketball coach and Curt Boswell, the principal of South Florence High School. I said, "Coach, you've been accused of calling one of your players a 'nigger.' Is this true?"

"Yes. I'm sorry. I know it was wrong."

"I agree it was wrong, and I'm going to suspend you for three days, without pay."

"Dr. Truitt, that's not fair. I work hard and these kids don't do their part. I pick them up and take them home. I go to bat for them with teachers, and I don't get much cooperation from them." Now crying, she continued, "I know what I said was wrong, but I was frustrated at the effort my team was giving in practice. They just don't appreciate what I do for them."

"I'm sorry, but that kind of language is not acceptable and cannot be tolerated."

Two days later I met with the board in executive session. We were meeting in the personnel conference room in the back part of the administration building, all nine board members crammed together in straight-backed chairs around a table. As I began telling of the latest name-calling incident, the breath went out of the room. Maggie Glover got up and left.

When I finished, Carroll Player asked about the coach's previous record. When I assured him there had been no similar incidents, he and most board members seemed satisfied with the way I had handled the incident. Maggie Glover, who had returned to the meeting, disagreed.

Glover moved to put the teacher on probation for a year. Larry Orr, a lawyer, reminded her she couldn't make a motion in executive session. I said I would monitor the coach during the remainder of the year.

Joe Carson, president of Investors' Savings and Loan, spoke up. "I think official probation is unnecessary. I'm satisfied that Dr. Truitt has handled the matter appropriately."

Glover said, "I think she should be fired."

Calvin Thomas said, "We need training for our teachers. I can't put up with this kind of stuff much longer. I don't know if I'll run for the board again."

At the March board meeting, Rev. W. P. Diggs, a college classmate of Martin Luther King Jr. and the acknowledged leader of the Florence civil rights movement, appeared before the board. Approximately sixty years of age, Diggs had gray hair and a big voice. When he spoke, he looked people in the eye, holding them with his gaze. Diggs wanted the SFHS basketball coach fired, calling her behavior unacceptable.

We seemed to be having an epidemic of name-calling incidents. The next month a cafeteria worker at South Florence High School, frustrated with the students, called a student a "black ass" and a "nigger." She was fired.

You might wonder why the cafeteria worker was fired and the teacher kept her job. Teachers have "property rights" to a job, meaning they can only be fired for cause and are entitled to due process procedural rights. While you might argue that teachers should be held to higher behavioral standards than cafeteria workers, this different legal standing has to be considered in firing a teacher.

Reacting to the racial name calling, the board, at its April meeting, adopted a new policy declaring racial or ethnic slurs unacceptable. The policy stopped short of mandating firings for violators, saying only they risked dismissal.

I worried about the new policy. While it was harsh in tone, it was vague. What does it mean to risk dismissal? In what cases would an employee be fired? Perhaps more important, the policy did not address the gap in attitudes about the calling of racial names. As evidenced by the basketball coach who thought a three-day suspension was too severe and the differences in how white and African American board members wanted to handle that case, people of different races were miles apart.

The policy did little to soothe resentment in the African American community. While both white and black school board members disapproved of the name calling, black members held a stronger view, firm in their belief that anyone guilty of such behavior should be fired. White members tended to opt for less severe punishment. As superintendent I realized I could not please everyone, no matter how I handled the issue. I only hoped we wouldn't have any additional name calling.

The name-calling incidents and the accompanying bad feelings could not have come at a worse time for the school district. In the spring of 1988, with the board campaigning to increase local taxes for operating the district, the name-calling incidents threatened the traditional support of the black community for school referenda.

The only district in South Carolina required to hold public referenda to increase operational taxes, Florence School District One teetered on the brink of financial disaster, drawing its reserve fund down to a zero balance to keep its schools open during the 1987–88 school year. Unless voters approved a tax increase, the district would be bankrupt at year's end.

History was against the district. It had not passed an operational referendum in ten years. Two votes had failed the previous year, partially because board members were divided in their support. But this spring the board united behind the referendum, voting 8–1 (with Weston Weldon dissenting) to ask for a 17.3 mill increase, a 25 percent rise in operational taxes.

With the school board leading the fight and the local chamber of commerce making the referendum's passage a priority, the prospects for success looked good. Still, the black vote was needed to achieve success.

The board's chair, Calvin Thomas, came to see me in April. "Tom, the NAACP is considering coming out against the referendum. Reverend Diggs feels the board should have fired the South Florence High School basketball coach."

"But Calvin, what about the new policy on racial slurs? Doesn't this show the board's good intent?"

"I'll remind them of the new policy, but I don't know if it's enough."

The next day, Calvin reported to me that Reverend Diggs was "moderately pleased" with the new policy, but the NAACP was still going to oppose the millage increase. I decided to call on Reverend Diggs. W. P. Diggs was pastor of Trinity Baptist Church, a large, influential downtown church. Although less active than in his younger days, he was still the recognized civil rights leader in Florence.

Diggs escorted me into his office, on the ground floor of the church, beneath the sanctuary. Since he knew why I was there, I immediately began my pitch.

"Reverend Diggs, I need your help in passing this millage referendum. The district has not had a tax increase in ten years. We're using $1.3 million from a reserve fund for this year's operating expenses. Unless we get this tax increase, the school district faces bankruptcy."

Diggs did not respond immediately. His stern, almost fierce, look made me uncomfortable. I squirmed and wondered if I was doing the right thing. Finally he said, "We've supported the district in the past, and what has it got us? You don't have any black assistant superintendents; black students are put in special education classes; and white teachers insult our children with racial slurs. Whites are not going to give us anything until we force it."

"Reverend Diggs, I'm interested in the welfare of all students. I don't deny there's been discrimination in the past, and we still have problems." I didn't want to get in an argument over past injustices. "Still, this is about the school district's need for operating funds. Unless we're successful with this vote, all children, black and white, will suffer," I said, ready to get on my knees and beg if I'd thought it would help.

Diggs never gave me a direct answer to my plea. I spent an hour with him, listening to his complaints against the school district and his defense of the NAACP's tactics. At the end of the conversation, I felt I had made some progress. Calvin Thomas confirmed it the next day, saying Diggs's support was lukewarm, but he would not oppose the referendum.

Although he was the most influential leader in the Florence black community, Diggs was not the president of the local chapter of the NAACP. David Lucas, a local realtor, held that office. One week before the referendum, Lucas called a press conference and announced his organization would not support the tax increase unless the district adopted an affirmative action plan.

I took no action. Lucas's timing made my decision easy. Had I wanted to accommodate him, I did not have time to devise and put in place such a plan. I worried less about Lucas after Calvin Thomas told me Lucas was acting on his own and was going to be reined in by the organization's members.

One week later I watched the votes being counted in the Florence County Public Services Building. The increase was going down in the early returns, but as the predominantly white districts reported, the "yes" votes increased. I later learned that some whites voted for the increase because I had not knuckled under to the demands of David Lucas. The final vote was 3,842 in favor to 3,094 opposed.

After the vote was counted, David Lucas came over to me and said, "Well, Doc, you beat me on this one." I just looked at him. He seemed to view the referendum as a personal contest. I didn't know what to say, and I turned and walked away.

Although pleased to have won the referendum, I was troubled by the racial aspects of the vote. I didn't want whites voting for the referendum because of a perception that I had stood up to the NAACP any more than I liked David Lucas trying to use the referendum to make political hay for his organization. With a school district approximately evenly split between black and white students, everyone had an equal stake in having a strong system. I was puzzled that the referendum had taken on a racial tone.

I was still learning about race and Florence School District One.

NINE **Palace Coup**

Calvin Thomas chaired the Florence School Board that hired me. An independent brick contractor, Calvin was active in community affairs. The second African American elected to the board, he had served longer than the previous black member and was the first African American to be elected chair, a post he had held since 1985.

Calvin relished chairing the school district board, and he did a good job. He presided over the meetings with authority, allowing other members to have their say while keeping the agenda moving. As the senior member of the board, he expected to remain chair. With seven white and two black members in a school district in which black students were 48 percent of the student population, the racial balance of the Florence board was out of kilter. Having Calvin Thomas serve as chair partially offset the underrepresentation of blacks on the board.

While the chair did not have more authority than other board members, he presided at meetings, which gave him greater visibility. The position enhanced Calvin's status and prestige in the community. The chair also served as the board's communication link to the superintendent, helping to plan meeting agendas and communicating board concerns to the superintendent. Although the chair served a one-year term, tradition prescribed that the board's senior member would serve as long as he or she remained on the board.

Carroll Player wanted to be chair. Living within a stone's throw of the Florence Country Club, Carroll viewed the more affluent parents of the West Florence area as his constituents. Bright and energetic, he loved being a board member and consumed school district information with the energy of an industrial-strength vacuum cleaner.

In May 1989 Steffanie Huffman, the district's public information director, came into my office, closed the door, and said, "I think you need to know this. Carroll Player is lining up votes to dump Calvin as chairman so he can be chairman. Don't ask me how I know, but I understand the votes are lined up. It's a done deal."

I was surprised and bothered by Stephanie's revelation. First, I was irritated to be hearing such information from the district's public information officer. Some board member was telling her something that he or she wouldn't tell me. Second, I knew how much Calvin valued being chair and didn't want to see him dumped unceremoniously. Finally, I was concerned about the impact of such backroom politics on board teamwork. The board was beginning to function as a team, but I could see Calvin's ouster destroying the fragile trust among members.

In spite of my concerns, I took no action. Superintendents who want to keep their jobs stay out of board politics. Even though I knew this change in leadership would damage the board in the eyes of the black community, I made no attempt to stop it.

When the board met the second week in May to organize for the coming year and I had not heard any more about the pending coup, I hoped that the conspirators had changed their minds. But, as I assumed the chair to ask for nominations, I had an unshakable sense of foreboding, as though we were about to open Pandora's box.

When I opened the floor to nominations, Miriam Baldwin immediately nominated Carroll Player, and I knew then that Steffanie's information was accurate. After Randa Everett nominated Lucy Davis and Mack Gettis nominated Calvin Thomas, the board elected Carroll chair by a 5–2–2 vote. Assuming the post, Carroll asked for nominations for vice-chair. Larry Orr nominated Calvin. When Calvin declined, Orr was elected vice-chair. Calvin nominated Mack Gettis for secretary. Lucy nominated Anna Rose Rainwater, who won by a 5–4 vote. The board, in a school district with a student population of 52 percent white and 48 percent black, now had only two black representatives and no black officers.

Trying to make Calvin feel better, at its next meeting the board adopted a new policy limiting the term of the chair to two years and making it clear that the position would rotate. While they never put it into writing, the board adopted what I called the "Rotary Club ascension model," where officers rotate from secretary to vice-chair and from vice-chair to chair.

In the eleven years I served as superintendent in Florence School District One, the ousting of Calvin Thomas as chair was the worst decision the board made. Calvin was hurt and angered, not only by the action but by the manner in which the change was made. Carroll Player lined up the votes (Larry Orr, Miriam Baldwin, Anna Rose Rainwater, and David Pate), knowing Calvin could do nothing about it. None of these five board members talked to Calvin about a change in the leadership.

Most whites in this country believe in majority rule, but whites are in the majority. We do not understand the feelings of minority groups, like African Americans, who can be denied rights, privileges, and opportunities by this same majority rule. When people vote based on race, those whose color places them in the minority can never win. This "palace coup" reflected the plight of blacks as a minority and the insensitivity of whites to this plight.

Calvin didn't get over it, and he became more bitter as time passed. As chair, he had worked to achieve the broader goals of the board and could be counted on to help resolve racial issues. After his ouster his agenda narrowed, and he refused to help mediate racial problems.

I don't know why Carroll Player and the other board members wanted to remove Calvin from the chair's position. My guess is that Carroll, who was immersed in school board work, just wanted to be chair. I doubt any of the board members who supported Carroll in this toppling of Calvin anticipated the havoc it would wreak for the school district.

The black community saw the change in leadership as a loss of influence. This election of school board officers in May 1989 marked the beginning of a steady deterioration in race relations in the school district that continued during the remainder of my tenure as superintendent.

Hindsight is supposed to be 20/20, but as I've reflected on this event, I'm still not sure what I should have done differently. As superintendent, I felt strongly that board members should stay out of administering the schools. I expected them to respect my turf. Conversely, I felt I should stay out of the board's election of officers.

I've asked myself if I would have done the same thing if the races had been reversed, if a black majority was trying to depose a white chair. I think I would have done the same thing—I would have stayed out of it.

Calling each other and lining up votes is regular practice for board members, especially when it comes to electing officers. The problem in this case was the insensitivity to the feelings of an African American. Several years later Calvin Thomas told me he was hurt more by the way it was handled than by the loss of the position. Ideally, the other board members should have talked with Calvin about their interest in rotating leadership. I'm not sure Calvin would have gone along with the concept, but I am convinced he would have been less bitter.

Another option would have been for me to confront Carroll Player about what I had heard. Again, I'm not sure whether I could have persuaded him to change his mind. I was afraid I would alienate the majority of the board without having any impact on the election of the chair.

Another alternative would have been to address the issue of the board leadership in an open meeting of the full board, not to address the move to oust

Calvin directly, but to engage the board in a discussion of the role of the chair and how he or she should be selected. Since I was not supposed to know about the coup, this would have been good strategy and would likely have given board members an opportunity to raise the issue of rotating leadership.

This strategy may not have changed the outcome of the election, but it would have prevented a total breakdown in board member communication.

Pouring Gasoline
TEN on the Fires

During the spring semester of 1991, a series of events acted as gasoline poured on the smoldering fires of racial suspicion and distrust. Problems that would have been difficult to solve under any circumstances became unyielding and intractable, mired in race.

On the first Friday in February 1991, I looked up from my desk to see Sara Slack, the assistant superintendent for personnel, and Evelyn Heyward, the principal of Lester Elementary School, walking through my office door. When Sara brought a principal to my office, it usually meant a sticky personnel problem.

"I take it you ladies don't have good news for me," I said.

"I'm afraid not," Sara said. "Evelyn has a problem with her secretary."

Evelyn jumped in. "You know how I've been worrying about money at the school, Dr. Truitt. It seems like we never have enough. I think I've figured out why. My secretary has been taking money from the soft-drink and cracker machines."

"Are you sure? How do you know?"

"Well, the Pepsi bill hasn't been paid in two months, and she admitted taking the money when we confronted her."

"Sara, do we have any idea how much she's taken?" I asked.

"No," said Sara, "but I think we need to have the books audited to determine what's been taken."

The secretary was a long-term employee of the district, well respected, a grandmother, and an active member of her church, but our investigation revealed she was also a calculating thief.

The cracker and Pepsi money were a minuscule part of the problem. For at least five years the secretary had been siphoning off student registration fees. Since the trail was cold and she'd been clever, we couldn't pinpoint the exact amount of her theft, but we were sure it exceeded ten thousand dollars. Since the money stolen belonged to the public, I knew we had to report the theft to the police and prosecute the secretary. In my board meeting agenda, I reported the incident to the school board and told them of my intentions to prosecute.

Before each board meeting, I sent a memo to the media explaining the agenda items along with my recommendations. The media memo excluded confidential information, such as the issue of the secretary.

The lead headline of the March 12, 1991, *Florence Morning News*—"Will the School Prosecute?"—caused me to choke on my shredded-wheat cereal. The newspaper story was about the secretary and the issue of prosecuting her. When I read the story, I realized it was based on the memo I had sent to the board the previous Friday. *How could the paper have gotten a copy of my memo?* I wondered. My mind raced. *Was there a Deep Throat in Florence School District One? Who could it be?* I couldn't imagine a staff member leaking such information to the press. I concluded the leak had to be a board member.

When I got to my office, I confronted Jerry Wilkes, my secretary. "Jerry, do you have any idea how the newspaper would have gotten a copy of my board memo?"

"They didn't get it from me."

"I'm not accusing you, Jerry. But they got it from somebody, and I want to know who."

An hour later Jerry appeared my doorway. "Calvin called," she said. "He's mad about the newspaper article. He thinks someone is trying to embarrass the Lester secretary."

Later that morning Pam McDaniel, who had replaced Steffanie Huffman as director of public information, came sheepishly to my office, and said, "Dr. Truitt, I know how the newspaper got the story on the Lester secretary."

"You do? How?"

"I gave my information packet to Karen Hatton," referring to the *Morning News* education reporter.

"And why did you do that?"

"Well, she came over on Friday wanting her packet, and I just gave her mine because I hadn't put the media packets together yet."

"That was a dumb thing to do."

"I know, and I'm sorry."

"You know that Calvin thinks someone's out to embarrass the Lester secretary, don't you?"

"Yeah, I know. I'll call him and explain what happened."

Pam, an African American, called Calvin and explained. After Calvin heard Pam's explanation, he knew that Pam's mistake was not a deliberate attempt to embarrass the secretary.

I was bothered though that Calvin didn't trust me enough to discuss the incident with me. I could see him shifting his role from being a board member concerned about the school district to one concerned about representing his constituency, which he defined by race.

The secretary was fired and prosecuted, but she never went to jail. The court required her to pay the money back and to provide community service.

A second incident occurred the same month and disrupted West Florence High School. Ironically, the trouble grew out of a Black History assembly designed to teach appreciation of African American contributions to American life. Students at West Florence had been assembled to hear speeches by two African American principals—Lionel Brown of Savannah Grove Elementary School and Clarence Alston of North Vista Elementary School. I had attended the assembly and was satisfied with the talks. But some of the African American students did not think the principals had shown sufficient passion for their subject.

Following the assembly, an African American female student had complained in her homeroom about the lack of fire in the speeches. A white boy in the class reacted by saying, "I wish all you blacks would go back to Africa." The female student told the boy "to go to hell," but later she also told her male friends about his comment.

At break time the next day, about forty black students in a tight group walked quickly through the commons area of the school. They didn't threaten anyone or break any rules, but white students felt threatened. Many panicked and left campus. Rumors of violence spread, and white parents began checking their children out of school.

Back in the sixties, when I was a junior high school principal in Burlington, North Carolina, student unrest was a major problem. My school had walkouts, sit-ins, and other disruptive behavior. I was so stressed by the events that I lost thirty pounds that spring. At times I didn't think I could keep going, but I felt I was involved in a noble effort to eliminate the dual system of schools—one system for whites, another for blacks—that characterized the South. I believed that if we persevered, relations between the races would get better. If someone had told me then that student unrest would still be a problem in the nineties, I wouldn't have believed it.

Even though no violence had occurred at West Florence High School, the situation festered, threatening to get out of control unless we could calm things down. Rumors were so bad that the city manager, Tommy Edwards, and the director of public safety, Ralph Porter, both called me and offered assistance.

When there are group confrontations, the groups have leaders. One way to stop the disruptions is to co-opt the leaders, but since the leaders are not always out front, it's not easy to identify them. But any principal worth his salt can identify the troublemakers in situations like this, and Alan Harrison, the West Florence principal, knew who was stirring the simmering pot.

Alan and I met with some other members of my staff and some police officers. We generated a list of probable leaders and designated adults to go to see these students at their homes. While the purpose of the visits was to ask the students to help quell the disruption, the visits also put the students on notice that we were watching them.

Police lieutenant Robert Ross, a large, imposing black man, volunteered to see some of the more militant black students. When Ralph Porter asked Ross what he was going to say to the students, Ross said, "There's some things you don't want to know." I was confident that Ross would deliver a clear message.

The next day I met with the West Florence administrative staff to plan for the coming week. When you have a large number of students violating the rules, it's tempting to make excuses for not following procedure, but we agreed to follow the normal procedure and suspend for five days students who left school without permission. We also eliminated the midmorning break for students, a time when students had free time and when problems occurred.

In an attempt to calm the public, I scheduled a press conference for Saturday to dispel rumors and discuss our plans.

The press conference was a disaster. WJMX, a radio station, announced the press conference as a public meeting. Some hysterical mothers showed up, including the mother of the boy who had made the "back to Africa" comment—along with her son.

I made a statement, emphasizing that there had been no violence, and explained the steps we were taking to insure student safety. One angry white mother got in my face.

"You're lying about what's going on at the school. The blacks are bullying the white students, and you're taking their side."

I listened but made little effort to calm her. She had to blow off some steam.

The other women left me alone, choosing to talk with Ralph Porter instead. I stood to the side and watched as Ralph talked with the women for several minutes.

On Sunday afternoon I met with Principal Alan Harrison of West Florence High and my top assistants. I asked the assistant superintendents to drop their normal duties and spend their days walking the halls of West Florence. We also had a constant police presence in the school. The presence of these additional adult authority figures, along with other changes, paid off, and by the end of the week the school atmosphere was close to normal.

As a follow-up, we asked Bill Newkirk, a black human-relations expert from North Carolina, to speak to the student body on Tuesday and to work with the faculty on Friday. Newkirk stressed communication and tolerance in his talks to both students and faculty. To establish a dialogue between black and white students, Alan Harrison also set up a biracial student committee to work on solving racial problems.

With things returning to normal at West Florence, we had survived the crisis but had not solved the problem. Experts, like Bill Newkirk, help in such situations, bringing a calming voice to schools involved in the conflict, but such intervention is like pumping up a flat tire without fixing the puncture. Similar problems will reoccur.

The incident at West Florence demonstrated how far apart blacks and whites were in the city. Efforts such as the Black History assembly, designed to promote understanding, had increased tension and resentment.

ELEVEN **Campaigning**

In this year of racial troubles, we also began struggling with how to accommodate the growth at Briggs, Royall, and Savannah Grove elementary schools. At the end of the June 1991 school year, the school board approved a bond proposal for $13.8 million to build the new middle school and a replacement school for Carver Elementary School and scheduled the bond referendum for September. I spent the summer promoting the referendum, but the community was not receptive to helping with the overcrowded schools. Other issues commanded their attention.

Florence County had just completed a property reassessment, resulting in higher assessed property values. The county notified people of the new value of their property in the summer. Because assessed values went up, most people assumed their taxes would also go up; but the law in South Carolina prohibits a government from increasing its revenue through property reassessment. Once the reassessment was complete, the county would be required to lower the tax rate so that the same amount of revenue would be generated. The county wouldn't set the tax rate until December however, after the bond referendum. This meant the board would be asking people to approve a bond for building new schools at a time when they thought their property taxes would be increasing.

A second problem was the new Florence County Civic Center building, which had been approved by city and county councils. The $20 million facility was going to increase taxes. People just didn't know by how much. The county was also building a new jail, derisively called the "Taj Mahal at Effingham," costing $11 million, more than most people wanted to spend to house criminals.

On August 8, 1991, less than six weeks before the scheduled referendum, I met with Lisa Wells, head of a graphics company; Rita McMakin, who ran an advertising firm; Jean Leatherman, wife of state senator Hugh Leatherman; and school board member Miriam Baldwin to plan a strategy for passing the referendum.

Rita said, "I've been talking to people about the referendum. They're not interested. I don't think it has a chance. If you were a paying client, I'd advise against proceeding."

Jean joined in: "I don't think I can raise any money for this campaign. I'm not getting a good response."

The following week the board postponed the referendum. I was disappointed but recognized that we had little chance of success had we proceeded.

A year later the community issues had receded into the background, and the board once again authorized a bond referendum. By this time the projected cost of the schools had risen to $14.3 million.

Once again I hit the campaign trail, which took me to a meeting with black ministers at Carver School in late August 1992. Accompanied by board member Miriam Baldwin, I asked for their support for the referendum. I expected the ministers to be receptive to our request. I was wrong. They had issues to discuss and were going to use them as leverage for their support.

One man asked, "What's going to be the name of the new school?"

Surprised by the question, Miriam and I looked at each other. We had not even thought of changing the name of the school. "The board has not discussed the name of the school, Miriam responded. "I've assumed we would continue using the Carver name, and I'm sure that's what other board members are thinking. I promise you I'll put the name issue on the September board agenda."

Another man asked, "Where is this new school going to be?"

We had not purchased property for the school for two reasons. First, we didn't want the community to think we would spend money to purchase land when we didn't have approval to build the building. Second, we didn't want the location of the school to be an issue in the referendum campaign.

I said, "We have not purchased any property for the new school and don't plan to do so until the referendum passes. I can tell you that we will build the replacement school somewhere in the current zone."

Larry McCutcheon said, "You don't expect us to believe that you're asking us to vote on building a new school without knowing where it's going to be located?" The nodding heads and rolling eyes of the other ministers told me that they agreed with McCutcheon.

After this exchange, the meeting went south, with the group grousing and complaining about a variety of school issues—the inadequate number of black teachers, how blacks were overrepresented in discipline cases and special education classes, and underrepresented in gifted programs.

Just when I didn't think I could stand it any longer, Julius McAllister, minister of the Mt. Zion AME Church, spoke up. "The referendum is for the children, and I will support it and will ask my church to support it." McAllister's statement turned the tide of the meeting. Several others indicated a willingness to look at the issue with an open mind.

The next day I wrote each minister a follow-up letter saying we would ask the board to endorse the Carver name and that the school would be built in the current zone.

With school year underway I spent much of September campaigning for the referendum. Lisa Wells and Rita McMakin joined forces to develop a brochure listing the prices of top-of-the-line athletic shoes and comparing the prices with the cost of the referendum. The slogan was "For the price of a pair of sneakers, you can give your child a better school system."

Where Do You
TWELVE **Put a School?**

As Dorothy Ellerbe and I celebrated the bond passage on the day after the vote, I was blissfully ignorant of the problems that lay ahead. With the money to build a replacement school in hand, I thought all other problems would be small stuff.

Before the referendum, the board had chosen the Key Collins firm as building architects but had not selected a site for the replacement school. With bonds in hand, site selection was the next step.

The Carver School neighborhood was densely populated with 80 percent of its students living within 1.5 miles of the school. Land for building a school was scarce and rebuilding on the present site was not an option since its six acres were less than half of the acreage required by state standards for a new school site.

Clemson University owned the only land in the immediate area with sufficient acreage to build a school. The university was willing to sell the school district enough acreage for a school, but it would not grant access to Highway 52 because of its plans for developing the site, forcing the board to buy property for an access on nearby Clement Street. Because only one landowner on Clement Street was willing to sell, access was limited to a long, narrow driveway, making the site look like a lollipop. With no other choices in the neighborhood, the board began negotiating with Clemson University for the property.

Trouble began a month later, in October 1992, when the architects met with Carver teachers, other staff members, and parents in interactive design sessions. In these sessions, architects work with clients to develop plans for the building. The process begins with a group discussion of desired features for the building. The architects then draw preliminary sketches and bring them back to the group for reaction. The process repeats until the group is satisfied with the plans, usually requiring three days to reach consensus.

When the architects first met with the Carver teachers and parents, the problem of limited access surfaced immediately. Teachers also raised safety questions about the proposed site, labeling the area as a hotbed of drug trafficking. Since the architects were also unhappy with the site, they accepted an alternative. From the second day of the interactive design process, the drawings placed the school on Stokes Road, four miles from the current Carver even though the board was committed to the Clemson/Clement Street property.

During one session a teacher asked board member Anna Rose Rainwater what might change the board's decision to purchase the Clemson/Clement Street property. Anna Rose suggested a petition to the board, and a week later the board received a petition with 593 signatures, asking that the replacement school be built anywhere but Clement Street. Of the 593 signatures, 80 belonged to staff members and 83 to Carver parents.

When other Carver community residents learned about the petition, they rallied in support of the Clemson/Clement Street property. Recognizing there was a controversy about the site, the board scheduled a public hearing for November 23, 1992.

The tables in the Carver cafeteria had attached seats, useful because they fold up with the table, leaving the floor clear for cleaning, but these small, round seats were designed for elementary children. On the night of the public hearing, the seats overflowed with adult bodies. Although additional chairs had been brought in, many people had to stand. Board members sat on the stage at one end of the cafeteria.

I favored the Stokes Road site for two reasons. First, I was concerned about limited access from Clement Street. Second, Stokes Road was the choice of the staff. Even so, I was willing to accept any site that could gain a consensus from the staff and the community.

I took the architect's drawings of the new school to the meeting, hoping the image of a new school would inspire people to compromise and reach consensus on a site.

I began the meeting by pointing out the two sites under consideration on a map. Chair Larry Orr then asked for public comment. Rev. W. P. Diggs was the first to speak. Diggs was angry, saying he had been betrayed by a promise to build the school in the same neighborhood as the current school.

Diggs was referring to the August 20 meeting when board member Miriam Baldwin and I met with fifteen black ministers. At that meeting I had committed to building the school within the current attendance zone, but the ministers, not understanding the Carver school zone was fifty square miles, had interpreted my comments to mean the same neighborhood.

Now in the public meeting, when Reverend Diggs told his followers that he had been promised the school would remain in the neighborhood, they believed him. It did not matter that I could document my statements about the zone with the follow-up letter I had sent to the ministers the day after the meeting.

The most heated exchange of the night took place between Rev. Larry McCutcheon, chair of the NAACP Education Committee, and Rosa Brockington, a computer operator at Carver. McCutcheon, an intelligent, well-respected man, said, "If the new Carver School is moved out of this community, they will send our children to North Vista, and they will never get to go to the new school. I know it will happen."

His comment pulled Ms. Brockington's chain because McCutcheon lived in the Carver attendance zone but sent his children to predominantly white schools, exercising the majority-to-minority transfer option. Brockington responded to him directly, "If you are not a part of this school, then you should not be involved."

I didn't question McCutcheon's right to speak, but his comment made me angry. I knew Carver children would not be sent to North Vista; such a move had never been considered. I wondered if he really believed it or if he was demagoguing.

By the end of the meeting, twenty-six people had spoken—nine preferring to build the new school on Clement Street; nine advocating moving the new school to Stokes Road. The other speakers were neutral on the site, offering general advice such as advising the board to consider the children.

One week later, on November 30, the board met to decide between the two sites. Chair Larry Orr gave each member a chance to comment, beginning with Doris Lockhart, the newest member of the board and one of two black members, but Doris, a woman who ran her own business, deferred.

Glenn Odom, a white lawyer with two children in the school system and a penchant for Mickey Mouse ties, spoke up. "I favor the Stokes Road site," he said. "When I look at the people advocating Stokes Road, I see teachers and parents. When I look at the people advocating Clement Street, I see people with no direct connection to the schools."

Randa Everett, a teacher and the mother of two children in the district, echoed Glenn's remarks. Dr. Carroll Player made it three in a row for the Stokes Road site, emphasizing the value of this site for long-term growth.

John Floyd, an insurance agent, and Miriam Baldwin, director of recruitment for McLeod Hospital, also favored Stokes Road but with reservations, each using the phrase, "if I had to vote tonight." When Calvin Thomas, president of the local NAACP and the other black member deferred, Larry, as chair, took the floor.

Larry, the one board member who consistently sought to resolve conflict, surprised me. "I am in favor of placing the school at the Clement Street site. My reason is my preference for neighborhood schools. Many people in the past have favored neighborhood schools in taking positions about busing. Clearly the Clement Street site is closer to where most of the children live and would result in less busing."

Calvin and Doris then joined Larry in support of Clement Street, with Calvin saying, "I'm warning this board. You need to listen to the black community."

Carroll challenged Calvin. "Who speaks for the black community? All of the people last week who spoke in favor of Stokes Road, except one, is black." Before the discussion could heat up and become personal, Larry stopped it, suggesting that other sites should be considered. The board agreed and planned to meet again in a week.

A week later I presented three additional sites. Two were on the north side of Highway 52, which heretofore had been considered a barrier because of heavy traffic. The board opted to visit the new sites before deciding—another delay.

At the regular board meeting three days later, even though board members had not visited the new sites, Calvin Thomas forced the issue, moving that the board select Clement Street as the site for the replacement school, citing the proximity of the site to the community and the absence of the need to extend busing. Doris Lockhart seconded the motion, which failed 5–3, with Larry Orr voting with Calvin and Doris.

The window of opportunity for purchasing the Clement Street site was closing. Clemson University, fearful of funding cuts if they received income from land sales, would not sell the land while the General Assembly was in session. If the board waited until the General Assembly adjourned, the opening of the school would be delayed another year. Florence schools closed for the winter break without a site being selected.

On January 22, 1993, a special meeting was called to discuss property for Carver School. John Floyd moved to purchase twenty-five acres at $10,000 per acre on Mechanicsville Road, one of the sites north of Highway 52 and three miles from the current location. The motion passed 4–2 with Anna Rose Rainwater, Randa Everett, and Larry Orr joining John in favor of the motion, and Calvin and Doris against. I hated to see the decision made with only four positive votes, but Carroll, Glenn, and Miriam, who were absent, would have voted for it. Larry, who had voted for Clement Street earlier, switched to Mechanicsville because Clemson was now saying it would not sell the Clement Street property.

The next day the *Florence Morning News* attributed the following to Calvin Thomas: "I feel like it was a slap in the face of the African Americans in the community for this board to make a move like that."

Opposition to the board's decision began to grow in the black community. On February 11, the *Pee Dee Times*, owned and managed by African Americans, ran an editorial saying:

> The obsession to move Carver Elementary School out of the black community to a very undesirable and inconvenient site is a part of Florence District One's continued efforts to preserve school segregation by preventing white children from attending schools in predominantly black areas.

The article stated that Leonye Cunningham and her son Dr. Roy Cunningham were circulating petitions to keep the school in the neighborhood.

On March 11, 1993, the *Pee Dee Times* reported that Roy Cunningham questioned the validity of the signatures on the petition gathered by the Carver staff and parents that advocated moving the school from the Clement Street area. According to the paper, the Florence NAACP, the Northwest Community Council, and the Florence Black Ministerial Alliance "have bandied [*sic*] together to fight the school move."

On May 5, 1993, the *Pee Dee Times* quoted Dr. Roy Cunningham as saying:

> At this juncture much of the responsibility for poor treatment of African-American children seems to be directly or indirectly on Superintendent Thomas Truitt and in the very near future we will be looking into the dismissal of Dr. Truitt although he will be given a chance to resign.

Several days later the group opposing the move from the Carver neighborhood sent a letter to the board asking for my resignation. Although the board did not seriously consider the request, it bothered me. Had my resignation come to a vote, Calvin Thomas and Doris Lockhart would have voted for it, knowing I had not orchestrated the site selection. I was angry that this Carver neighborhood group, claiming mistreatment themselves, would be so unfair.

The board was split. Tension filled each board meeting like an explosive gas. If anyone had lit a match, the room would have exploded. Calvin, senior member of the board and president of the NAACP, felt no one was listening to him. White board members thought Calvin was demanding too much and was insensitive to the needs of the majority community.

Trying to heal the rift, I planned a team-building retreat for the board during the weekend of May 9–10 at Florence-Darlington Technical College. I asked Dr. Dudley Flood, an African American and former North Carolina assistant state superintendent and the man who, in 1967, had given me my first training in black-white relations, to lead the team building.

The school site issue was not resolved at the seminar, but the board members began airing their differences. Some healing occurred. Then someone lit the match.

Two days after the retreat, I was notified by mail that the NAACP had filed suit against the Florence School District One Board of Trustees and me. The location of Carver was the main issue, but the suit raised other issues—the shortage of black teachers, the overrepresentation of black students in the special education program, their underrepresentation in gifted classes, and the racial imbalance of the schools. The NAACP had contacted the U.S. Justice Department and had asked them to intervene in Florence. Calvin Thomas, president of the NAACP, had participated in a team-building retreat, knowing this suit had been filed—and had said nothing.

Calvin had to play his cards close to his vest. He knew about the lawsuit, but he could not tell other board members about it without betraying the NAACP. Other board members felt, as Calvin had when he had been ousted as chair, that they had been blindsided.

On May 19, the board held a special meeting and voted 6–1 "to hold in abeyance moving forward with the agreement to purchase the property on Mechanicsville Road during the pendency of law suit 4-93-1134:2." John Floyd, in a fighting mood, voted against the motion.

Even though I had been a superintendent for eighteen years, my lack of experience in building schools was affecting my ability to lead. Naively, I thought a school board had a right to pick a site for a new school and didn't think our board had done anything wrong.

I had been taught to seek solutions to problems that were "win-win" for the persons involved. In this case I could not find a solution on which the different groups could agree. Leaders of the NAACP, who favored the Clement Street site, were saying we had ignored the community. Carver teachers and parents supported moving the school out of the community, being adamantly opposed to building on Clement Street.

The U.S. Justice Department responded quickly. On June 8, Michael Maurer, a Justice Department lawyer in his thirties, visited the school district, bringing with him Kelly Carey, a school-zoning expert. I took them to the Clement Street site.

From his first viewing, Maurer didn't like the Clement Street site. Rather than push the site issue, Maurer turned his attention to student attendance zones and faculty assignment issues. He told us immediately to reassign faculty members to achieve racial balance in each school. Recognizing that changing school zones is a more complex issue, he put us on notice that he expected us to begin working on a plan to reassign students to eliminate racially identifiable schools.

On August 16, 1993, board attorney Laurence McIntosh, assistant superintendent for fiscal services Gerald Holley, and I met with fourteen representatives of the NAACP to negotiate the Carver School site issue. After a brief discussion, we piled in our cars and journeyed to Clement Street to look for other possibilities for building on that site. When we were looking at the site favored by the NAACP, several in the group who had spoken in favor of it didn't know where it was. Reverend Diggs, without seeing the absurdity of the question, asked me, "Where is that site where we wanted to put the school?"

Facing a long and costly lawsuit and hoping to avoid rezoning, the board caved in and agreed to settle the suit on two points: it would put the school on Clement Street, and it would pay the attorney's fees—over forty thousand dollars —for the NAACP. The board officially approved this settlement on October 7, 1993, in a special meeting by a 6–1 vote. John Floyd was still in a fighting mood.

A Whitewashed Election

When invaded by a grain of sand or a parasite, an oyster secretes a fluid called nacre that gradually encloses the foreign object and forms a pearl, one of the world's most valued gems. Motivational speakers use the oyster example to suggest that we can convert problems into pearls. We had a lot of irritants, but I was never able to turn any of them into pearls.

South Florence High School, the largest of the three Florence high schools with about 1,600 students, sits off Highway 52, the old Charleston Road. Its students come from the more rural part of the school district. During my first week in Florence, one South Florence parent proudly proclaimed, "We're the redneck high school."

In October 1993 an African American student was turning around in her seat, talking to a girl sitting behind her. The white teacher, who had taught English at the school for years, walked over and placed her hand on the girl's shoulder.

The girl jumped up and yelled, "You hit me. I'm going to tell my mother."

Three days later the South Florence principal, Curt Boswell, called me and said, "Dr. Truitt, I need to tell you about an incident." Boswell went on to tell me the girl's mother was taking out a warrant against the teacher for assault, claiming that the teacher had hit her child.

"I've interviewed every student in the class," Boswell went on. "Nobody supports the girl's version of the story. Everyone says the teacher just touched her on the shoulder."

"Well, why is the mother bringing assault charges?" I asked.

"She believes the girl. She thinks we're all racists. But the worst thing is that the teacher is going to be arrested. I've called Sheriff Gregg and made arrangements to have the teacher go to the jail, be charged, and be released."

"That's crazy," I said. "Why is she being arrested if there's no evidence against her?"

"In South Carolina, all it takes is for someone to file a charge and law officials are obligated to make the arrest," Boswell said. "Dr. Truitt, this is a bad situation. I don't want this girl here any more. I've suggested to the mother that she might want to transfer her."

A day later I was relieved when the mother came to me and asked that her daughter be transferred to West Florence High School. Recognizing that she could not go back to the South Florence English class, I granted the request.

On the day the girl was scheduled to enroll at West Florence, the mother again showed up at my office, saying she had changed her mind and wanted her daughter to remain at South Florence. She had taken her daughter to South Florence, but Principal Boswell had refused her admission, telling the mother she would have to talk with me before the girl could come back there.

I said, "When we last talked, you asked for a transfer to West Florence, indicating you didn't want your daughter to go back to South Florence."

"I know, but she doesn't want to go to West Florence. She wants to stay at South Florence."

"What do you think is best for her?"

"I'd rather have her go to West Florence."

"Then that's what I think we should do."

The mother enrolled the girl at West Florence. I worried that the girl would have trouble at there, too, but she graduated a year and one-half later without any serious incidents.

Even though the case against her was absurd, the teacher had to defend herself in court, incurring personal expense. Several months later the case was heard in magistrate's court before a jury of six people. Several witnesses testified that the teacher had only laid her hand on the girl's shoulder. No one corroborated the girl's version. The jury found the teacher innocent in less than ten minutes. When the verdict was announced, the girl let out a big wail.

October 1993 wasn't a good month at South Florence High School. In addition to the incident in which the teacher was charged with assault, a serious fight took place in an art class. A white student threw some clay at a black student, who then beat up the clay thrower, bloodying his lip and giving him a serious black eye. School officials decided the white student had started the fight by throwing the clay. Since board policy required suspension for willing participants in a fight, both were suspended for three days.

The white student's mother went into orbit: she couldn't understand why the other student was not expelled. She came to me and demanded his expulsion. I acknowledged that her son was the loser in the fight but pointed out that he was responsible for starting the fight by throwing the clay.

She didn't want to hear it. She declared violence was a problem in the schools and went on a one-woman campaign against it, writing a letter to the editor and calling people. She was getting little response until the newspaper featured her in an article and publicized her plea for people to come to the November board meeting.

The crowd at the board meeting was a little larger than usual, but when public participation began, only three people, including the woman on the campaign, spoke about school violence. The first speaker was unemotional, saying parents need to be more involved and that she planned to volunteer at the schools.

The second speaker shocked the crowd (and me), alleging that her five-year-old son had been molested with three teachers in the room. I had no idea what she was talking about and wondered how something like that could happen and I would not know about it. The next day I learned that a little girl had put her hands in the pants of this woman's son, who seemed to enjoy it. While incidents like this don't happen frequently in kindergarten, sexual exploration is not unusual among young children. Rather than make a big deal of the incident, the teacher had written notes to the mother asking her to tell the boy not to let the little girl do this. After talking with the mother of the little girl, the teacher had considered the incident resolved.

The mother whose son had been beaten in the classroom was the last speaker. According to her, her son was attacked from behind without warning. She failed to mention that her son had thrown a piece of clay at the other boy. She kept asking, "Who is responsible?" confusing responsibility and liability. When Chair Larry Orr tried to explain this to her, she cut him off. She continued to gripe and complain until Larry called time on her.

The publicity surrounding this event had created the feeling in the community that our schools weren't safe. To deal with the issue, I recommended that the board appoint a biracial committee of students, parents, teachers, and principals to study school safety, but before the committee could meet, a major fight, involving eleven students, all black, disrupted Southside Middle School. Nine students were expelled because they would not stop fighting when school officials came to break the fight up.

Parents panicked. Three middle school mothers came to me. Concerned about the safety of their children, each was considering taking her children out of the public schools.

A week later the board expelled an eighteen-year-old student from Wilson who had shot someone off campus the previous weekend. He claimed self-defense but was expelled by a 5–2 vote, with Doris Lockhart and Calvin Thomas, the board's two black members, voting against his expulsion.

Whether a school board has the authority to expel a student for off-campus activities is a gray area. In this case the board felt the student's violent act was so serious that he represented a threat to other students in school. Calvin and Doris voted against the action, saying they didn't feel the board had authority to deal with off-campus behavior. I wondered what their vote would have been had the student killed the student he shot.

At its February meeting, the school board, reacting to the series of violent incidents and unwilling to wait on the School Safety Committee report, toughened its policies on student misbehavior. Henceforth any student who brought a knife or gun to school would be expelled, no matter how small the knife and even if the knife never came out of the pocket. A student who attacked a fellow student without provocation would be expelled. Any time there was a fight, the police would be called, and the participants taken to jail.

The board passed these rules by a 6–2 vote with Doris Lockhart and Calvin Thomas voting against them. Lockhart's and Thomas's votes against both expelling the shooter and the stricter rules indicated a difference between black and white board members on how order was to be maintained in the schools.

In addition to the pressures of dealing with student discipline problems, the school district had major financial troubles. In the spring of 1994, we projected a budget shortfall of $2 million. We had two choices: make serious cuts in our budget or ask the public to vote for an increase in taxes. The board opted to ask the voters for the increase. On the last Monday in April, the board invited the public to the "Annual Meeting" required by law. Held in the Poynor Adult Education Center auditorium, the meeting had two parts: an explanation of the budget and a school board candidate forum.

Poynor Adult Education Center is a historic building, three stories high with white columns in the front, that formerly served as the city's junior high school and now houses the district's adult and community education programs. The Poynor auditorium, including the balcony, seats about three hundred people. At the front of the auditorium is an elevated stage with burgundy curtains. When I presented the budget, there were no questions from the crowd of about twenty-five people.

After the budget presentation, the board candidates took the stage. Three incumbent board members—Calvin Thomas, Anna Rose Rainwater, and Glenn Odom—were running for reelection against a half dozen challengers. Each candidate made a short opening statement and then responded to questions from the audience.

Board member Carroll Player, sitting in the audience, asked each how he or she stood on the millage increase. Carroll, a supporter of the millage referendum, was trying to get each candidate to go on record as supporting the millage increase. Carroll's ploy backfired as every candidate, except one, supported it. Dick SoJourner, an oral surgeon, said he was against it.

Because of the small crowd, SoJourner's statement would not have mattered if the newspaper had not reported it the next day. As the only candidate opposed to the millage increase, he was elected on May 3 when the voters turned down the request for a tax increase. Glenn Odom and Anna Rose Rainwater were reelected, but Calvin Thomas, the board's senior member, was defeated, leaving the board with only one African American member. Carroll Player's question at the forum probably changed the racial composition of the board. Had Carroll not asked that question, Calvin probably would have been reelected.

Later that month, responding to NAACP complaints about the location of the replacement Carver School, lawyers from the U.S. Justice Department came to town and told us to reassign teachers for the coming year and to develop a plan for bringing racial balance to the schools' student bodies for the following year. The board transferred the teachers and committed to developing a plan for bringing racial balance to the schools.

Searching for a Site

FOURTEEN

"Tom, I've found a site." Laurence McIntosh, the board's attorney, was on the phone.

"Laurence, what are you talking about?"

"I've found a site for the new Carver School."

"Laurence," I said, "we've settled the lawsuit with the NAACP by agreeing to put the school on Clement Street. What do you mean you've found a site? Are you suggesting we break our commitment?"

"No, no, no, but I think this site will be acceptable to the NAACP. It's located on Cashua, behind the Clemson property we wanted to buy. The location is ideal, still close to the Carver neighborhood, but accessible to white parents whose children will be transferred to the school. Since there are no houses around it, there's no stigma to the neighborhood. It's owned by Nucor Steel, and they are willing to sell."

I could tell Laurence had been busy. "That sounds too good to be true," I said.

"There is one problem. The cost is $25,000 an acre."

I paused. The board had only budgeted $8,000 an acre to purchase land for the new building, but if we could find a site acceptable to both white and black communities, the price of the land would be worth it.

I shared Laurence's good news about the new site with the board, which agreed to invite NAACP representatives to a meeting in July 1994 to discuss the new site. Because all board meetings are public, the date and purpose of the meeting had to be publicized.

After the meeting was announced, calls began pouring into our office asking for details. I called the board's chair, Anna Rose Rainwater, to tell her of the interest in the meeting.

"Tom," Anna Rose said, "I think we should move the meeting from the boardroom to the Poynor conference room. We're not going to have space to hold this crowd."

I agreed with Anna Rose and asked Jerry Wilkes, my secretary, to notify the media and Calvin Thomas, president of the Florence NAACP, of the change in meeting place.

The next morning Jerry came into my office and said, "Calvin called me last night. They're not coming to the meeting."

"What do you mean they're not coming to the meeting?"

"He told me the NAACP is not coming to this meeting. They don't like the change in the meeting place. They think it's some kind of setup."

Surprised, I asked, "Did he understand why we changed the meeting place?"

"Yes, but he still thinks it's some kind of setup."

I called Laurence McIntosh and told him what had happened. Laurence, who had served twenty-five years as the school board's attorney, and Calvin, who had served on the board for twenty-two of those years, knew and respected each other. Laurence volunteered to call Calvin and work it out.

When distrust is so high that you can't get people to come to a meeting, you know you're going to have trouble communicating. In this instance Laurence was able to persuade Calvin and other NAACP representatives to come to a rescheduled meeting.

Less than a month later, representatives of the NAACP, accompanied by their lawyers, attended a meeting in the Poynor conference room. Laurence McIntosh showed the delegation a map of the new site and explained to everyone how it would be more accessible than the Clement Street site. The NAACP representatives were receptive to the new site, but they asked for one consideration. They wanted the board to develop a way for students in the Carver community to walk to the back of the school property. Since this walkway would not require students to cross any streets, the board agreed to the proposal.

After gaining agreement on the site, Chair Rainwater asked NAACP representatives if they had any suggestions for how the board might develop a plan to balance student assignments in the district. Speaking for the delegation, attorney Brenda Reddix-Smalls said the NAACP would accept any plan approved by the U.S. Justice Department.

The board then voted unanimously to acquire the Nucor property.

But the attempt to relocate the school seemed cursed. Before the board could purchase the Nucor property, the South Carolina Highway Department erected a roadblock, revealing plans to build a highway through the middle of the property. Laurence McIntosh urged the board to proceed, saying the Highway Department would not condemn a new school, but Hamilton Lott, Nucor's chief executive officer, vetoed the deal. If a school were in the way of a highway, the Highway Department would divert the road and take more of his remaining property. Once again the board was looking for a school site.

In September 1992, when we had passed the bond referendum, I had told Dorothy Ellerbe, principal of Carver School, that we would have a replacement school for Carver before the middle school was built. Two years later we were opening the new middle school—Sneed, named for former superintendent Henry Sneed, but we still didn't have a site for the replacement Carver School.

But Dorothy had her new school, being named the first principal of Sneed Middle School. Cynthia Young, whose position as the district's director of instructional improvement had been eliminated in the spring budget cuts, took over at Carver.

FIFTEEN **Flawed Firing**

North Vista Elementary School had no white students. Like Carver, it was located near town. Most of its students walked to school. Even though the student body was all black, the faculty was approximately 50 percent black, 50 percent white.

Dr. Clarence Alston, an African American and the principal of North Vista, spoke so softly you had to strain to hear him, but he used corporal punishment to keep students in line. African American parents and teachers spoke highly of Alston. White teachers were more guarded in their comments, not criticizing him but rarely praising his leadership.

Alston seemed uncomfortable with white people. He once told me that he would like to have more black teachers at his school, even saying he would be happy with an all-black staff, claiming that white teachers can't teach black students.

At the end of the 1993–94 year, Alston wanted to fire a white teacher. Missing one eye and suffering from a hearing loss, the teacher lacked peripheral vision and slurred her words. Alston said she couldn't control her students.

I was nervous about Alston's recommendation—his documentation was weak, and I knew the board would be sympathetic to a handicapped teacher—but in spite of these doubts, I supported his recommendation. I had given him responsibility for running the school and felt I needed to back him. Additionally, I knew other administrators would be watching the proceedings. I did not want to be accused of failing to support a principal.

The board heard the teacher's appeal in August 1994.

Clarence Alston was the only witness on the first night of the two-night hearing, testifying for three hours, responding to questions from the teacher's attorney and the seven board members sitting as a review panel. Listening to the questions and Alston's answers, I could tell board members were trying to find holes in Alston's case.

On the second night two teachers testified for the teacher, praising her competence. Since teachers do not evaluate other teachers, I assumed their testimony would carry little weight with the board. Speaking in her own defense, the teacher's narrative made Alston look bad. She described how he communicated with her through notes, even sending her a note that he was going to recommend her dismissal, rather than talking with her face-to-face.

When the hearing ended at 10:00, the board adjourned and scheduled a meeting the following week to consider the case.

The next day board member Anna Rose Rainwater called. "Tom, I've just received a call from the husband of a North Vista teacher. He's not a happy camper. He told me that Clarence Alston called in the two teachers who testified at the hearing and chastised them."

Fifteen minutes later Anna Rose called back, saying, "Tom, this thing at North Vista is getting worse. Mrs. Morgan* just called me to complain about Dr. Alston calling her on the carpet. I told her to see you this afternoon after school." Mrs. Morgan was one of the teachers who testified on behalf of the dismissed teacher.

That afternoon Mrs. Morgan and her husband came to my office. Mrs. Morgan, speaking through clenched teeth and holding her husband's hand, said, "Dr. Truitt, I'm very upset. Dr. Alston called Mrs. Shelly† and me into his office and gave us what-for for testifying at the hearing. Martin Schmid and Debbie Watson were right there when he did it." Schmid and Watson were assistant principals.

I knew Alston's confrontations with these teachers guaranteed we'd lose the case. I could understand his being upset with the teachers, but his calling them in on the carpet did nothing but validate the dismissed teacher's account of his autocratic style. The following week the board's 6–1 vote to reinstate the teacher bore out my expectations. It also reflected the racial composition of the board members present. Doris Lockhart, the only black member, supported Clarence Alston and voted for dismissal.

After the board voted to reinstate the teacher, they asked me to stay. Several board members asked me what I was going to do about Alston's mishandling of the dismissal. Board members were particularly angry about Alston's calling in the teachers who testified on behalf of the dismissed teacher. Outnumbered, Doris Lockhart didn't say anything.

The next day I met with Alston. By the end of our conference, we agreed that the timing of his meeting with the teachers was lousy and that he should have handled it differently. He agreed to schedule new meetings with the teachers to begin reconciling his relationships with them, even saying he felt it was his responsibility as principal to do so.

---

* Not her real name.
† Not her real name.

Later in the week Alston and I met with Mrs. Morgan, who had requested the meeting, her husband, and Thad Daise, a young black man who wore bow ties and was the South Carolina Education Association representative for teachers in our area. The critical point in the conference came when Daise asked Alston, "If you had it to do over, would you do anything differently?"

Alston said, "I wouldn't hold conferences with these teachers at the same time."

Daise responded, "You mean you wouldn't change anything about the way you handled the dismissal?"

Alston said, "No."

Mrs. Morgan said, "I would like to be transferred to another school, and I think Dr. Alston owes me an apology."

I said, "I'll think about the transfer and let you know. The apology is up to Dr. Alston." I was hoping Alston would offer some concession, but he was silent.

Mrs. Morgan, her husband, and Thad Daise left, indicating that they would be filing a grievance.

Even before Mrs. Morgan asked for a transfer, I knew that she and Alston could no longer work together. But before I could grant her request for a transfer, I had to consult with Sara Slack, the assistant superintendent for personnel, and find a suitable placement for Morgan and the other two teachers. The three were transferred to other schools, where they successfully taught for several more years.

Clarence Alston's attempt to fire the white teacher and my support of him, his subsequent attempt to intimidate the other white teachers who testified at the hearing, and the transfer of these white teachers from North Vista at a time when we were being forced by the Justice Department to balance faculties raised concerns about North Vista School. Until this time the focus of our discussions on rezoning had been on the replacement Carver School. From this point on, North Vista would become more of an issue.

SIXTEEN   Public Meetings

In August the board had directed me to begin developing plans for bringing racial balance to the schools. I assigned the responsibility for developing these plans to Rick Reames, the assistant superintendent for student services. Rick, a trained school psychologist whose responsibilities included overseeing student personnel services and special education, had been with the district since the late sixties and was our resident attendance zone expert. After Rick developed eleven different plans for balancing the races in the schools, we were ready to go public.

The public meeting was held on September 27, 1994, in the Poynor Adult Education Center auditorium. The board, Rick, and I sat on the stage, and Rick presented the eleven alternatives to an audience of two hundred frowning people.

Although we identified eleven plans, each was a variation or combination of two approaches—rezoning and pairing. In rezoning, school attendance lines are redrawn, requiring some students to change schools. In pairing, attendance lines are not changed, but two schools are combined into one zone and the grade levels are adjusted. For example, you might pair two K–6 elementary schools—one predominantly white, the other predominantly black—creating a larger, racially balanced zone. One school might be assigned grades K–3, while the other would serve grades 4–6.

Since this meeting was to provide information for the board and the public, we did not take public comment, nor did we ask the board to evaluate the different options.

After this meeting I contacted Dr. Gordon Foster, director of the Southeastern Regional Desegregation Assistance Center, who arranged for Rick and me to visit Port St. Lucie, Florida, where a new desegregation tool, controlled choice, was being implemented. Controlled choice gives parents a choice of schools but limits options to maintain racial balance. The plan seemed to be working in Port St. Lucie, but I had my doubts about Florence. Too many Florentines opposed any kind of change.

At the second public meeting, held on October 4, Rick and I described controlled choice. After our presentation, the board invited members of the audience to speak. Twenty-four people (twenty-two of them white) spoke at the meeting. Recurring themes were none of the plans are acceptable; don't be afraid of the Justice Department, fight them; and solicit parental involvement. City councilman Rick Woodard advised the board that a committee of parents, Concerned Citizens for Excellence in Education, had been formed to study the issue.

We learned more about this group from a former teacher, who called Rick Reames after the meeting. The group had about four hundred members, all white, including two lawyers and former board member Lucy Davis. With a "throw-the-rascals-out" attitude, the group did not support the board or me, blaming us for the problems of desegregation.

When the board met again, on October 6, Rick presented two plans—one that required rezoning and one based on controlled choice. Again the public was allowed to comment, and again the majority of the audience and of the speakers (twelve of fourteen) were white. No one spoke in support of either plan. I was bothered that blacks were not attending the meetings in the same numbers as whites or speaking up at the meetings. With whites dominating the public discussion and with eight whites on a nine-member board, the meetings were as one-sided as a cheating husband's explanation.

A week later the Justice Department gave us a deadline of November 18 by which to submit a plan for resolving racial imbalance.

Dr. Foster came up from Miami and met with the board at the October 26 meeting. Foster said there are two mandatory options for desegregating schools —rezoning and pairing—and two voluntary methods—magnet schools and controlled choice. Board members Miriam Baldwin and Glenn Odom also reported on their trip to Massachusetts, where they had observed three school districts that had implemented controlled choice. Both Glenn and Miriam were enthusiastic about controlled choice, but the public didn't buy the idea. Of the twelve people who spoke at this meeting, only Jean Leatherman spoke favorably about the concept.

By this time several people were speaking to the school board at every meeting, emerging as the leaders of the parents. Dr. Seth Smith, a physics professor at Francis Marion University; Billy Isgett, an optician; Dr. Joe Moyer, an allergist who had done his undergraduate work at West Point; and Nancy Rawl, a mother of middle and high school children, were frequent spokespersons for the white parents.

James Williams, an elder in the True Life Faith Fellowship Church, and William McAllister, president of the North Vista Elementary School PTA, spoke up for the black community. They chastised the white speakers for advocating resistance to the Justice Department and spoke frequently of "doing what's right."

Most speakers, while angry about the possibility of rezoning, were civil. One white mother and frequent speaker, however, was particularly obnoxious, turning her back to the board to play to the crowd as she spoke.

Most board members kept their cool, but on this night, Glenn Odom lost it. "If you don't like our schools, you can just pull your children out and put them in private schools," Odom blurted out.

As soon as he said it, Glenn knew he had made a mistake and quickly apologized, saying, "I'm sorry, but I'm tired of our schools being criticized and attacked. We're doing the best we can, and we need your support."

At a meeting on November 1, Rick presented two options for controlled choice. Although the concept was not well received by the community, the board directed the administration to refine one of the controlled choice plans for consideration at the next meeting. The board also requested a rezoning plan with three intermediate schools serving grades 5 and 6. These plans were presented in a meeting on November 7. Neither received support from the sixteen people who spoke during the public participation.

At this meeting the board took an unorthodox step: it invited the public to submit recommendations. Until this time public participation had been limited to speaking at the meetings; the board had not appointed any advisory committees.

While inviting the public to make recommendations may have seemed like a good strategy to increase acceptance of the eventual plan, only one group had come to the meeting prepared to make recommendations. By asking for public recommendations, the board was legitimizing the parent's group—an all-white one—that had formed.

Dr. Seth Smith, representing the Concerned Citizens for Excellence in Education, stepped forward and presented his plan. Using data acquired from our student database, Smith had crafted a plan that already had the endorsement of the organized parent group. Making North Vista a magnet school was the distinguishing feature of his proposal. The magnet school would serve the entire school district and would attract students by offering a special program. With parents volunteering to send their children to the school, the district could select students in a manner that would provide racial balance. For this plan to work, the new Carver School would have to be enlarged to accommodate additional students.

At the regular board meeting on November 10, the board dropped the controlled choice concept and scheduled another meeting for November 15 to discuss the "Parents' Plan," as Seth Smith's plan was now being called.

The board invited Seth Smith to come to the stage again at the November 15 meeting, where he presented the latest version of his plan. Similar to his previous proposal, the revision still projected North Vista as an alternative or magnet school and an enlarged Carver. Since the plan required a larger Carver School, it could not be implemented until the fall of 1996.

About four hundred fifty people attended this meeting, the most we'd had. Thirty-nine people spoke that evening, with seventeen speakers supporting the Parents' Plan. Clearly it was the people's choice.

Although the plan had the momentum of a rockslide, not everyone embraced it. County councilman Terry Alexander, an African American, spoke against the plan, accusing Seth Smith of "protecting his neighborhood."

With the Justice Department deadline looming, the board met the following night and voted to submit the Parents' Plan to the Justice Department. The vote was 7–2, with Dick SoJourner, because he didn't want any change, and Doris Lockhart, who didn't think the plan went far enough, voting against it. At the end of the long, tense meeting, Anna Rose Rainwater thanked the public for coming and, in a weak attempt at humor, said she would like to see "most of them back" for future meetings.

After the meeting Elder James Williams confronted Anna Rose. He had taken exception to her comments, interpreting them as racially motivated. Anna Rose, who had probably been thinking of the woman who turned her back to the board and played to the crowd, apologized, saying her comments had no racial intent.

The next day I got a call from a North Vista parent, who asked for a meeting with the board about the closing of North Vista. He had not attended any of the previous meetings and now wanted the board to hold a special meeting for him. I told him the board was not meeting on this issue again until we heard from the Justice Department.

The plan submitted to the Justice Department required rezoning 41 percent of the elementary school students, changing attendance lines for all elementary schools except North Vista, but made no changes in middle and high schools. Nevertheless, later in the week, the *Florence Morning News* ran an article stating the board had decided to rezone the middle and high schools.

Anna Rose called me at 8:30. "Have you seen the story in this morning's paper? My phone started ringing off the hook at 7:00 and hasn't stopped since."

I called Denise Pridgen, a reporter at the *Morning News*. "Denise, where did this story come from? The board has made no decision about middle and high schools."

"Glenn Odom and Doris Lockhart both told me that the board would address middle and high schools," Denise responded.

"Well, the board has done nothing with middle and high schools and comments by two board members do not represent board action. You need to run a correction on this story."

Even though she didn't like being challenged, she ran a correction on Saturday.

On Friday, the day before publishing the new article, Denise called me again. "I've heard the Justice Department has rejected the board's plan. What can you tell me about that?"

"Denise, I haven't heard a thing. Sounds like a wild rumor to me. I doubt the Justice Department has even looked at our plan yet."

Denise called Michael Maurer to ask him about the rumor. When she ran the correction on Saturday, she mentioned that the rumor wasn't true—a strange inclusion in her article.

A large contingent from North Vista Elementary School attended our December meeting. Several addressed the board, but the North Vista contingent had not done their homework. Most did not know the board plan, including the part calling for North Vista to become a magnet or alternative school. Many in the audience murmured and mumbled throughout the meeting.

One speaker began by saying, "Let the words of my mouth and the meditations of my heart be acceptable in Thy sight, O Lord, my Strength and my Redeemer." She talked on and on. Believing prayer was the answer, she said, "The worst thing we ever did was to take prayer out of the schools."

The meeting lasted so long that we decided to postpone the regular meeting.

While the board was struggling with a rezoning plan, the staff continued to look for a site for the replacement Carver School. Once again Laurence McIntosh, the board's attorney, located an alternative site, this one between Sumter Street and Cashua Drive. The property had two problems however. It was expensive, beyond the board's budget, and it was on the other side of Cashua, meaning that students walking from the Carver neighborhood would have to cross busy Cashua Drive to get to school.

The board could reduce the cost by purchasing a limited amount of frontage on Cashua Drive (the most expensive part of the property) and more land in the back. Even so, the price was $650,000 for thirty-one acres—more than four times the amount budgeted for the school site.

The location problem was more difficult to solve. When asked about the Sumter/Cashua site, the NAACP countered with a site off Harmony Street, nearer the Carver neighborhood. Like the Clement Street location, this property was isolated and would require major road construction, making it even more expensive than the Sumter/Cashua site.

Gerald Holley—the assistant superintendent for fiscal services—and I met with Calvin Thomas to explain the problems of Harmony Street and the reasons the board preferred the Sumter/Cashua property. He said he had no problem with the property, but that he couldn't speak for the NAACP board.

That night the school board, including Doris Lockhart, now the only African American on the board, voted 8–0 to purchase the Sumter/Cashua property.

The board had waited as long as it could. Further delay in acquiring a site would mean the school could not open for the 1996–97 school year, when a rezoning plan was anticipated. Since a rezoning plan would send white students to Carver, the location of the new school was critical.

The next day I wrote Calvin Thomas, notifying him of the board's action and asking for the NAACP's approval of the purchase. I didn't get a response from him, but I was encouraged when the *Florence Morning News* quoted Calvin as saying:

> It's (the Sumter/Cashua site) within our scope. We felt like it should be connected to the community. I'm in the process of trying to set up a meeting with my executive board to get their feeling on it.

On February 27, 1995, the NAACP met but took no action on the Sumter/Cashua site. On March 6, the NAACP Executive Board unanimously rejected the site, notifying the school board in writing and sending a copy of the notification to its attorney. Even though the NAACP acted on March 6, I did not receive news of their action until March 9, the same day the *Morning News* printed an editorial, "Carving Slowly on Carver." Referring to the NAACP leadership, the editorial said:

> The ones most guilty of fanning the flames of delay are now the very ones who first called the fire department. Come on folks, let's quit the political jockeying here. No one appointed the NAACP keepers of the District One domain. It's a joint effort, or at least it's supposed to be.

The board met on March 14 to respond to the NAACP's rejection of the Sumter/Cashua site. The board directed Laurence McIntosh and me to send a letter to Calvin Thomas and Rev. Larry McCutcheon, explaining why we were proceeding with the purchase. The next day we drafted the letter and mailed it.

Several days later Dick SoJourner called. "Dr. Truitt, do you mind if I release your letter to the press?"

"You have that right," I said.

Almost immediately after I hung up, I had second thoughts and called Anna Rose Rainwater, who chaired the board. She didn't think sending the letter to the press was a good idea, and I tried to stop Dick. I was too late. He had already made his deliveries.

On March 18, 1995, the *Florence Morning News* ran an article explaining why we had rejected the Harmony Street site. Three days later the weekly *News Journal* printed the entire letter. On March 30, the *Morning News* published an editorial, "Little Harmony Seen Coming from the NAACP," saying, "Shame on you, NAACP. Do you really ever want harmony?" Two days later Calvin Thomas was quoted in the *Morning News* as saying he was not going to talk further to them unless they changed their attitude about the Carver site.

On April 3, Laurence McIntosh told me he had received a letter from the NAACP's attorney that said either put the Carver School on Clement Street or a site of their choosing, or they would take us back to court.

That night, at a scheduled school board meeting, the chair asked each member what he or she wanted to do. All, except Doris Lockhart, said to continue with the purchase of the Sumter/Cashua property. If we did not, we wouldn't be able to open the new school by 1996. Time was running out.

SEVENTEEN　Working with Justice

Early the next morning, the day after the board agreed to purchase the new Carver site, Laurence McIntosh called.

"Tom."

Although he had only said my name, his tone told me he had important news. "We've heard from the Justice Department," I said, sensing the reason for his call.

"They've rejected the board's plan," he said.

"What did they say?"

"I really haven't had time to study their response, but I'll bring you a copy right over."

Knowing that the community had been waiting anxiously for word from the Justice Department, I said, "Laurence, I don't want to sit on this. Are you available this afternoon for a press conference?" I was ready to go into a press conference unprepared rather than delay the release of information so important to the community. When Laurence said yes, I notified the press that we would be holding a conference at 1:00 P.M. on the Justice Department response.

Usually attendance at press conferences in Florence was limited to representatives from both Florence television stations and the *Morning News*. But on this occasion, one television station announced the press conference on its noon news show, and a good-sized crowd was on hand for the announcement. City councilmen Billy Williams and Ed Robinson, county councilmen Terry Alexander and Herbert Ames, parent activists and future board members Billy Isgett and Nancy Rawl, and several staff members and parents showed up, as did most of our board members. I expected the board's chair, Anna Rose Rainwater, to preside at the conference, but she sat in the back, leaving the meeting to Laurence and me.

I announced, "The Justice Department has rejected our proposal for rezoning and has sent us a counterproposal. While we have not had time to study their proposal, they are clearly stating that the issue will be resolved if we accept their offer."

The Justice Department plan proposed no changes for North Vista Elementary School, leaving it an all-black school. Additionally, it proposed increasing the white percentage at Delmae from 70 percent to 80 percent. Both proposals were surprising since the Justice Department had ordered us to eliminate racially identifiable schools.

I liked the proposal to maintain the present lines for North Vista. This school had frustrated our plans to achieve a racial balance because its densely populated neighborhood was all black. With North Vista out of the mix, balancing the other schools would be easier.

I didn't like the rest of the Justice Department plan since our plan provided better racial balance in other elementary schools. Their plan also proposed rezoning middle and high schools, moving Windsor Forest and Grove Park, two affluent white neighborhoods located within a stone's throw of West Florence High School, to Wilson High School. If the Justice Department's intent had been to promote private high schools, it couldn't have adopted a better strategy.

The Justice Department plan smothered the community like a big, wet blanket. The sale of houses screeched to a halt, and the realtors hated us. No one wanted to buy a house until the school rezoning issue was settled. We couldn't tell anyone where their children would go to school in the coming year.

Just when I thought things couldn't get any worse, the NAACP filed suit against the Florence School District One Board of Trustees, asking the board to establish single-member districts. Although the authority to change the board system of representation resided with the General Assembly, the Florence One School Board was the named defendant in the suit, a move designed to recover attorneys' fees for the plaintiff.

If a single-member district plan were implemented, the composition of the board would change radically since the majority of the board lived in the same part of town. I wondered if I had made a mistake in not pursuing a chance to return to Virginia. A month earlier Guy Yeatts, former assistant superintendent for finance in Danville, had called me in his capacity as superintendent search consultant for the Pittsylvania County Schools, the county that surrounded Danville. While Guy couldn't offer me the job, I felt comfortable that if I had wanted it, it was mine.

I had decided not to pursue the job for two reasons. First of all, I didn't want to be a quitter: I wanted to see the Florence rezoning and school construction through to the finish. Second, my wife was not interested in returning to Virginia since our only son had settled in Columbia, South Carolina.

Feeling insecure, I called Anna Rose Rainwater and told her how I felt. She listened sympathetically. That night she called me at home and said, "Tom, I've been thinking about this situation, and I want you to know that anyone not wanting to renew your contract will have to go over my dead body." I slept better after her call.

A week later, on April 17, 1995, the board met for its first discussion of the Justice Department proposal. Since the Poynor auditorium was not available, the meeting was held at the Moore Intermediate School auditorium to accommodate the large crowd that was anticipated.

Meeting in executive session before the public meeting, board members vented their frustrations. Some didn't like the idea of leaving North Vista all black even though it helped with the racial balance in other schools. They thought the Justice Department plan gave the black community what it wanted while ignoring the white community's wishes. Some white board members saw the black community getting to keep its neighborhood school, while white students were being forced to change schools. They didn't understand that leaving the school all black was not what the black community wanted. The black community did prefer this option to making North Vista a magnet school, seeing that as a ruse for eventually closing the school, but their first choice would have been to integrate North Vista by bringing in white students.

During a discussion of the single-member district suit, Doris Lockhart complained, "Blacks can't get elected under the present system."

Randa Everett blew her top. "You could get elected if you would do the work like the rest of us who have been elected to the board. Put out yard signs, knock on doors, put up billboards, and get your people out to vote."

Doris, recognizing Randa's anger and the futility of arguing, said nothing.

The open meeting was held in the school auditorium. Board members, unsmiling, looking like prisoners of war, sat on the stage. For most of the meeting, they lambasted the Justice Department but did not comment on the merits of the Justice Department proposal. Finally, after an hour of posturing, they directed the administration to develop an alternative plan that would retain North Vista's current zone. The vote was 7–2 with Doris Lockhart and Dick SoJourner voting against the proposal, she because she wanted to see North Vista integrated and he because he wanted to keep every thing the same.

The proposed changes made no one happy. Whites favored leaving school zones alone. Blacks wanted the schools integrated but didn't want to bear the burden of the process. They wanted to see whites bused to North Vista.

When people are unhappy, they look for someone to blame, and in this case, I had a bull's eye on my back. The following Sunday the *Florence Morning News* published a letter written by Elder James Williams calling for my resignation.

I wasn't about to resign, and I resented the letter. I was trying to solve a problem, one that had hung over the community for more than twenty-five years, dating back to an unresolved lawsuit in the early seventies. I had not created the problem, and I didn't like being blamed for it.

On May 3, 1995, the board met to discuss the Justice Department proposal. About one hundred fifty people, most veterans of the fall public meetings, assembled in the Poynor Adult Education Center auditorium.

A group of white speakers railed against the Justice Department and encouraged the board to fight the Justice Department plan. Billy Isgett called the board's case "fightable, defendable." Seth Smith, the author of the Parents' Plan, asked the board to consider hiring a legal expert on desegregation and offered to raise $2,500 for the first visit.

A small number of white speakers resented the North Vista zone being left intact. Dr. Joe Moyer, who had just lost a bid for a seat on the school board, said that the North Vista Education Committee plan should be made public. Mike Wallace encouraged the board to consider making North Vista a magnet school as an option to leaving it all black. Amy Haynes, a senior at South Florence High School and the fourteenth white speaker at the hearing, summed up the view of the white contingent when she called the Justice Department plan "garbage."

Elder James Williams, William McAllister, and Charles Foxe of the North Vista Education Committee (NVEC) had requested that they be allowed to speak last. As Elder Williams approached the microphone, a murmur like distant, rumbling thunder spread through the predominantly white crowd.

Williams began, "I am saddened by the suggestions I've heard here tonight to fight the government. Don't you folks read the papers? Don't you know that Darlington County just spent a pile of money fighting the government and lost?

"Some of you say it's unfair for North Vista to remain all black. Where were you these last twenty years when it's been an all-black school? I didn't hear anything from you then.

"I don't want the school to remain all black, but I'd rather leave it that way than have it become a magnet school, which is just an excuse to close it down."

Next, Charles Foxe chastised the earlier speakers for their insensitivity to blacks. Responding to comments about blacks not participating, he offered, "Blacks are not going to participate when they feel they're not going to get a fair shake."

At this point Foxe turned his back on the board and faced the audience. "It's a slap in the face of the black community to be willing to bus North Vista students to white schools but not the reverse." Promising to remain involved, Foxe concluded, "I will be here. I will be watching."

After William McAllister and Rev. James Brown echoed the remarks of Williams and Foxe, board members responded.

John Floyd said he was so stressed his fillings were falling out. John said he was tired of being castigated for so many things over which he had no control.

Joking about his position on the right of the stage and the political spectrum, Dick SoJourner said he favored neighborhood schools. Dick said we were dealing with socioeconomic problems that the schools cannot solve. "It's life, and we're not going to change it," he concluded.

Glenn Odom asked a few questions without taking a position. Miriam Baldwin joined those in bashing the Justice Department saying, "They're fighting us."

Randa Everett, whose board term was expiring in a couple of weeks, said she understood the feelings on both sides of the issue.

Picking up on Randa's compromising tone, Carroll Player said, "We need to work toward a logical solution to the problem and figure out the best plan for the community."

Doris Lockhart commented, "The board needs to address the middle and high schools."

When Larry Orr began his comments by saying, "We don't have consensus . . . ," Anna Rose interrupted, "Boy, are you quick."

Larry went on. "I propose a meeting with Michael Maurer of the Justice Department to seek clarification regarding the proposal." Larry's comments drew immediate, warm applause from the audience and agreement from his fellow board members.

At 10:30 the next morning, I went to Laurence McIntosh's office. In his law library with its three walls lined with book shelves, we called Michael Maurer. He declined our invitation to meet with the board and said he would prefer to react to a proposal. Laurence said he would call him back.

While Laurence was talking with Maurer, board chair Anna Rose Rainwater had walked in.

Stymied but needing to take a step forward, I outlined a strategy I had been formulating for some time. I suggested that we offer Maurer a magnet plan for middle and high schools. If Maurer agreed, we could tell the community that middle and high school lines would not change, perhaps softening their resistance to making changes in the elementary school lines.

Anna Rose and Laurence liked the idea. Laurence called Maurer back and handed me the phone.

After an exchange of pleasantries, I told Maurer, "Our middle and high schools are not far out of balance. Your proposed plan to rezone them is like an initiative for a private high school. Private schools are already springing up like dandelions. Your proposal would cause us to lose more white students and ultimately hurt the efforts to bring racial balance to the schools. With magnet programs, we can achieve racial balance without upsetting people. We'd like for you to consider the International Baccalaureate program as a magnet for Williams Middle School and Wilson High School."

Maurer didn't reject the idea, but he said he would need more specifics. I agreed to get him something within three weeks, and Maurer committed to coming to Florence during the second week in June.

When I hung up, Anna Rose said, "For the first time in a long while, I feel some optimism. We may just get through this thing."

I was pleased with the conversation, feeling I had won some concessions with hope of even more.

North Vista
Education Plan

EIGHTEEN

Earlier in the spring I had begun meeting with three black parents (William McAllister, James Williams, and Charles Foxe) and three white parents (Seth Smith, Nancy Rawl, and Chris King) in an attempt to find a compromise plan that would satisfy the community. After the initial meeting we expanded the group to include Rev. Larry McCutcheon, chair of the NAACP Education Committee; Tommy Cooper, director of secondary education; and principals Allie Brooks, Clarence Alston, Julie Smith, and Curt Boswell. On the afternoon of my call to Michael Maurer, I met with this group.

At 3:30, the beginning time for the meeting, none of the black leaders was present. I called William McAllister and found him at home, confused about the meeting time. While I was talking with McAllister, Charles Foxe walked in, relieving me of the anxiety that I had misinformed the black leaders about the meeting time. McAllister promised to call Elder Williams and come as soon as possible. As we were beginning the meeting, Reverend McCutcheon walked in.

I told the group about my call to Michael Maurer, emphasizing our plans not to change middle and high school lines. Relief flooded across Nancy Rawl's face since her children were in the middle and high schools. I then pointed out that our plan was essentially the same as the one accepted by the community with the exception of North Vista, which remained intact.

Seth Smith asked Clarence Alston, principal of North Vista, "Do you want the school to remain all black?"

After Alston talked for about five minutes, I still didn't know the answer to Seth's question. Tommy Cooper spoke up and said, "I can assure you I don't want to see it remain all black."

From that point the discussion covered the usual racial issues—the number of black teachers, the performance of black students, the conditions at predominantly black schools, and other such topics. Several times during the meeting, white participants asked questions about the North Vista Education Committee's plan.

William McAllister, the chair of the NVEC, refused to make the plan available until Charles Foxe prevailed upon him to do so. I made copies of it, but as they were being passed around, McAllister changed his mind, saying he was not comfortable sharing the plan.

Speaking directly to McAllister, Chris King said, "I don't like being teased. I'm giving my time here and missing my work at General Electric. I have a lot of things I need to be doing and could be doing in the time I'm spending in these meetings. I'm going to be honest with you and expect you to reciprocate and trust me." Larry McCutcheon followed up and pleaded with McAllister to share the plan. It did no good.

In spite of the failure of the meeting, the group agreed to meet again the following week. Seth Smith, still pushing the magnet school concept, said, "If the group is interested I'd be willing to put together some information on magnet schools for your consideration."

Larry McCutcheon responded, "I'm willing to look at it." The three members of the NVEC said nothing, and I interpreted their silence as a good sign. At least they weren't speaking against it.

A couple of days later I got a call from Denise Pridgen of the *Florence Morning News* asking about a teacher survey at North Vista. I knew nothing of a survey, but the next day Sara Slack, the assistant superintendent for personnel, told me that Clarence Alston had surveyed his teachers regarding the plan to leave North Vista all black. I called North Vista, but Alston wasn't in. I called again the next day. Alston was at a kindergarten graduation.

Before I could get in touch with Alston, I got a call from board member John Floyd saying that Billy Isgett, head of Concerned Citizens for Excellence in Education, had complained to him that Alston had called in six teachers and "screened" them for the proposed plan. According to Isgett, the teachers, feeling threatened and intimidated, had taken their grievances to the newspaper. In complaining about Alston, Isgett also alleged that, earlier in the year, a teacher at North Vista had been hit by a child with no disciplinary action being taken.

Less than fifteen minutes after John hung up, the husband of a white North Vista teacher called. He had earlier called John Floyd, who had referred him to me. According to the husband, Alston had called his wife in, told her she had a bad attitude, and made a vague threat against her.

Later, when Alston came to see me, he showed me his appointment book, which identified eight people he had talked with during the last two days. Of the eight, six were white teachers; the other two, black teacher assistants. The wife of the man who called me was one of the teachers.

Alston said, "These conferences had been scheduled for some time and are part of a process I've undertaken to talk with every staff member. I wasn't screening for the North Vista plan. I didn't even mention it in any of the conferences. Furthermore, I don't know anything about a child hitting a teacher during the year."

"We've got a problem, Clarence," I said. "I'm going to ask Randy to talk with the teachers to hear what they have to say." Randy Koon was director of elementary/middle schools.

"I want to be present when he talks with them."

"I think Randy better talk with them alone."

The year before, when we had been required by the Justice Department to move some black teachers from North Vista and replace them with white teachers, Alston had complained about having to take the white teachers. "Clarence," I had said, "If you insist that only black teachers can teach black kids, the corollary of that position is only white teachers can teach white kids, and we're back to segregation." "That's not true," Alston responded. "Black kids are different. They have special needs."

Two important meetings were held on May 17. The parent discussion group met to review Seth Smith's plan, and the board met to hear a report on the NVEC plan. Dr. Isaiah Reid, a professor at South Carolina State University who had served as a consultant to the North Vista Education Committee, would present the committee's plan.

On the night of May 16, James Williams called me at home and suggested we cancel the meeting of the parents, saying it was too much to meet at 3:30 and then present the NVEC plan at 5:30. Williams said Charles Foxe was unable to come and McAllister was doubtful. I encouraged Williams to contact McAllister, get him to come, and proceed with the meeting. He said he would call me in the morning if he couldn't work it out. He didn't call.

About twenty minutes before three, Reverend McCutcheon called and canceled out of the meeting, saying he had an emergency. At 2:50, McAllister called and said Dr. Reid was with him and would be coming to the meeting. I said, "Bring him along."

We began the meeting with Seth Smith presenting his plan for a magnet school. Under this plan, all students would attend North Vista by choice. There would be no students zoned to the school. The idea was that the school would be so attractive that parents would volunteer to send their children there.

Tommy Cooper asked, "What will happen if we try the magnet school and it doesn't work? Will you then be willing to rezone North Vista?"

Seth answered, "It will work."

Elder Williams said, "We focus too much on shifting bodies without raising standards for students who attend the school. I think we need to concentrate on improving curriculum."

Seth said, "Test scores have soared in the Bartow Elementary School, a magnet school in Savannah."

The group explored the possibility of having the gifted and talented program at North Vista with a group of neighborhood students who would get the special attention of the NVEC plan. At one point Clarence Alston asked why we were focusing on North Vista and suggested that we look at some of the other issues. I disagreed, saying North Vista was the issue.

Near the end of the meeting, Chris King pointed out that if the magnet school did not work, we would have the board plan by default.

Later Dr. Reid asked if Dr. Alston would be in charge of the gifted and talented program. I waffled on the answer but had made up my mind about mixing the two plans. I didn't think Alston would work well with the parents of gifted children.

As the time for the board meeting neared, Elder Williams asked, "Do we have consensus on the plan?"

I was surprised at the question since no one had indicated support for the plan. Julie Smith said she could accept the NVEC plan, and I said I could support either one. No one else budged.

I asked if we should meet again. Charles Foxe said no, and no one disagreed with him.

Then the whole group, with one exception, moved across the hall to the boardroom where Dr. Reid was to present the NVEC plan. Clarence Alston just disappeared.

Dr. Isaiah Reid had been working with North Vista Elementary School as a consultant. About sixty-five years old, Reid let the board know he was a honors graduate of Boston University and had attended Harvard, where he made all A's.

According to Reid, the North Vista Education Committee plan revolved around extended time. Students would stay at school ten or twelve hours a day and eat three meals at school. Parents would be trained to help their children and would be employed as assistants to help in the after-school program. Only teachers who wanted to be at North Vista would teach at the school. Dr. Reid said the percentage of black teachers at the school would have to be increased for the plan to work.

The plan called for students to wear uniforms and be taught alternative ways of resolving conflict. A special summer program enabled young scholars to spend summers at Cornell University, which was cosponsoring the program through Dr. Josephine Allen, a professor there. Dr. Reid estimated that the plan would cost $1.5 million a year but said that the plan would be financed with grants.

The board liked the plan. Why not? It justified leaving North Vista an all-black school, and it cost nothing.

After the board finished questioning Dr. Reid, Reverend McCutcheon, who had come in shortly after the meeting started, asked if the audience was going to be able to ask questions. Some board members wanted to open the discussion up to the small audience, but Anna Rose, who had said at the beginning of the meeting there would be no audience participation, stuck to her guns. She set another meeting—May 29, Memorial Day—to have public discussion on the NVEC plan.

Fewer than one hundred people attended the Memorial Day meeting. Dr. Isaiah Reid sat on the Poynor auditorium stage with the board members, between John Floyd and Dick SoJourner, the board's two most conservative members.

After explaining that the purpose of the meeting was to provide an opportunity to question Dr. Reid, Anna Rose recognized a man in the audience. The man wanted an explanation of the plan before he asked a question. Repeating that the purpose of the meeting was to ask questions about the plan, Anna Rose told the man she would come back to him and called on Nancy Rawl.

Rawl, the mother of two teenage children, had attended all the public meetings related to the rezoning issue. She asked, "Dr. Reid, who is responsible for the coordination of this program and for funding it?"

Reid answered, "A strategic management team at the school will coordinate the program. We will seek five years of grant funding for the program."

Nancy Scott, a regular speaker at the meetings, asked, "How will the $1.5 million make a difference when a concentration of Title I money has not? I also question the viability of having teachers work twelve-hour days."

Reid disagreed. "Title I has made a difference. The school has been making steady progress. Teachers will not be expected to work twelve-hour days. We are going to train parents for the extended-day responsibilities."

Mike Wallace, a member of the Concerned Citizens for Excellence in Education and an advocate of a magnet program for North Vista, verbally sparred with Reid. Wallace pushed the issue of extended time and asked how the plan addressed desegregation.

Reid deflected the question on extended time, saying too much emphasis was being put on this aspect of the plan. He said the district was losing too many black kids and this plan would help them compete. "It is a research-based program," Reid concluded.

Wallace kept pushing. "Is it going to help integration?"

Reid responded, "It addresses the problems of North Vista."

Wallace maintained, "It has nothing to do with the Justice Department demands."

"Yes, it does."

"I'm not understanding. The school is 100 percent black."

"I am interested in solving the problem, not busing children."

"Does it deal with the current problem?" Wallace asked.

"Do you have a problem with a school doing this?" Reid demanded.

"If it is fair to leave North Vista alone, it is fair to leave all schools alone."

At this point Anna Rose intervened: "The purpose of this meeting is to ask questions about the NVEC plan. Please confine your questions to that topic."

Wallace, took a parting shot, "We need to raise up all schools. This plan doesn't address the issue at hand."

Elder James Williams was next. He talked about money, saying he hoped the district would not be "exclusionary" in funding. I had no idea what he meant. Williams added that the NVEC plan addressed many of the issues identified by the Justice Department.

Melinda Graham Pringle was the first black to challenge Dr. Reid. "What's going to attract the parents to the school?" she asked. "They're not coming now."

Reid responded by saying, "If you don't come, there will be other parents there. Suppose North Vista offered you ways to advance yourself, three meals a day, five days a week?"

Pringle responded, "I am opposed to the plan and to leaving North Vista all black."

Rev. Larry McCutcheon said, "I feel there is a need to clarify what happens in the after-school hours. What are students going to do then? I would think homework and recreation would be worthwhile."

Rick Ayers, the white man who had declined the invitation to speak first, now advanced to the microphone. "I have volunteered in the schools for eight years," Ayers said. "And I don't see much participation by black parents."

"I object to that statement," McCutcheon blurted from the audience.

Ayers shot back. "It looks like glorified babysitting to me."

Russ Fortier, the husband of a North Vista teacher, sounding like a caller to a radio call-in show said, "I have four questions I want to ask. I'll ask them and then sit down and listen to your answers." His questions were (1) Do you have a model somewhere else that you could point to? (2) Is this the first effort of its kind? (3) How are you going to deal with the additional staffing needs? The homework center fizzled out because there was not sufficient staff to keep it going. (4) Is your program going to knock kids out of participating in baseball and other recreational activities?

Reid answered, "Bamberg School District Two has a similar program with total community involvement, as does Milwaukee, Wisconsin. There will be a research component to the program, including follow-up of the junior scholars. We haven't completely designed the recreation program, but I expect to have tennis, golf, and even a swimming pool."

Fortier, who had not sat down, asked, "If it works, will it be open to all students?"

Reid said, "It will have to be."

Natasha Dowdy, a reporter for the *Pee Dee Times*, was upset with Ayers's comment about the lack of participation by black parents. Ms. Dowdy said, "This is a stereotypical point of view we will have to get over. My mother was an active volunteer the whole time I was in school."

William McAllister, chair of the NVEC, came forward to ask Reid some soft-ball questions. "Have you seen parent involvement increase at North Vista in the last three years? Have you seen improvement in test scores? Do you think the plan will attract parents?" McAllister went on to say he has been inspired by the plan and hoped to become an educator, perhaps a science or physical education teacher.

Reid said parents had overflowed the school at recent meetings. He expressed hope that the plan will help parents become more skillful in helping their children.

Catherine Fulton, a North Vista parent, was the final speaker. Defending the plan, she said, "What's good for one should be good for all." I was not sure of her meaning, but I think she was saying that black students are shortchanged in the district. Expressing her concern that too many children are on the street, she said, "Let's do what we can to help a child."

Anna Rose now asked if any board members had any questions for Dr. Reid. Everyone looked at Carroll Player, who always had something to say. He didn't disappoint. Carroll wanted clarification on the extended day issue. Reid made it clear that extended day staff would be added, saying no teacher can be effective for a ten-hour day.

Carroll next addressed the survey that had been conducted at the school the previous week. Sixty percent of the teachers had said they were not interested in working in the school under the plan. Carroll asked Reid how he would over-come this resistance.

"I'm a change agent," said Reid. "Any time you make changes, there will be resistance. Teachers need to want to teach at North Vista. We need to look at the affective domain. If there is incongruity in the attitudes of teachers and the cur-riculum of the school, achievement and behavior will suffer. We may need more African American teachers at North Vista. I assume we will need some more."

"Where will we get the teachers?" asked Player.

Reid replied, "I have contacts all over the state through people I have trained. These people will help me find competent African American teachers."

Dick SoJourner asked how long it would take to train parents to be teachers in this program.

"Four years," was Reid's answer.

Dick expressed disbelief, but Reid said again it could be done in four years.

Dick then turned to the issue of paying for the strategic management team, making it clear he felt they should not be paid. Reid said he felt entitled to con-sultant fees, but he was not interested in pay for the strategic management team.

Shifting gears, SoJourner commented, "I can't see leaving black students iso-lated for six years. My common sense tells me it is best to begin integration at the first grade."

Reid responded, saying, "In studying organizational behavior, we have looked at dependency and counterdependency. We want students to be independent, but social isolation in the classroom hurts the self-concepts of black students. We want them to feel good about themselves. Sixty-eight percent of the inmates in South Carolina prisons are black males. Something is wrong. We must discover what it is, pinpoint it, and get rid of it."

SoJourner now wanted to know where Reid planned to put the swimming pool. Reid said there was quite a bit of space at the school but didn't specifically locate a spot for the pool.

Dick's final comment was that the program sounded like "glorified babysitting."

Doris Lockhart wanted to know how long Reid had been working with North Vista and how he had been funded. Reid said, "Since 1990," and with some help from Clarence Alston in the audience, "and with a Target 2000 grant."

Lockhart then gently chided board members for raising the funding issue, saying other schools had been given permission for special projects without being scrutinized. She warned the board to be careful if it wanted the community involved.

"I'm in an awkward position since we've already voted to keep North Vista all-black," Doris said. "I'm against all-black schools."

Larry Orr interrupted. "I must have been asleep when we voted to keep North Vista all black because I don't remember a vote. I have not committed to North Vista remaining all black. Of course, I'm a lawyer, and lawyers are not committed to anything."

Orr then asked Reid about the Bartow School in Savannah, which is part zoned and part magnet school for the gifted and talented, asking if such a program would be workable with Reid's program. Reid responded by saying his doctoral students had looked at the Bartow School and found that it did not enhance the performance of the local students.

"It's a school within a school," Reid said. "Bartow does not address the problems of black students. They still have the same problems."

Orr followed up. "Is the program predicated on 100 percent African American students?"

"Not predicated on 100 percent African Americans. It just happens to be located in such a community."

John Floyd, mentioning that he was married to a teacher, offered that teachers would have to want to be there for the program to work. He said that teachers who didn't want to be a part of the special program should be offered equal job opportunities elsewhere. Reid agreed.

Carroll Player went back to the Bartow School, saying, "The principal there says the resident population has benefited from the program. Test scores are now in the average to high range for black students."

Reid said he would have to see the test scores.

The meeting had been going on for ninety minutes. Anna Rose decided to end it. "Thank you for going through this process. The board is facing a grave decision. We will be meeting tomorrow night at 7:00 in the boardroom. The meeting is adjourned."

NINETEEN Board Decision

The next night, when the board met to decide on a response to the Justice Department, I dared to hope we were nearing the end of the process. The board had spent all year working on a plan for elementary schools, operating on the premise that middle and high schools would fall into place once the elementary plan was set. But we still didn't have a plan for the elementary schools. I decided it was time to shift the emphasis to the middle and high schools.

The Justice Department proposal to change middle and high school lines was ridiculous. Wilson High School attendance lines were moved to Hoffmeyer Road, literally within sight of West Florence High School.

As an alternative to changing attendance lines, I had begun thinking about a magnet program for middle and high schools. If we could implement a magnet program at Williams Middle School and Wilson High School that would attract white students to those schools, we would not have to change attendance zones.

After some research, I chose the International Baccalaureate (IB) program as the program most likely to attract white students to Williams Middle School and Wilson High School. The IB program has high standards and quality control, requiring students to demonstrate competence on a comprehensive examination to earn an IB diploma. Additionally, IB students have to write an extended essay of at least three thousand words, perform community service, and do three hours of homework daily.

During the public hearings, I had been silent, taking notes and listening. At this meeting, I decided to lead.

"I've sat quietly through most of these meetings," I began. "Tonight I'm going to talk a lot.

"I propose we offer the International Baccalaureate program at Williams Middle School and Wilson High School. If the program is successful in attracting students, it will solve our problems of racial balance in the middle and high schools."

Doris Lockhart asked, "What makes the IB program more attractive than the Advanced Placement courses?"

I responded, "IB has an international focus and is considered a level above AP. Many of the workers at Hoffmann–La Roche are coming from other countries. They will not want their children to lose their second language." Hoffman–La Roche was the newest industry in town.

Doris shifted the focus to race: "In other words, 80 percent of the students we will attract will be white, leaving it another exclusive program in the district. Am I not correct?"

I said, "Principals at Williams and Wilson indicate they have students who will participate in the program, and these students will diversify the racial composition of the total program. Also, the program will be open to anyone with an interest and an aptitude."

After a few more questions and comments, John Floyd asked if Anna Rose wanted a motion.

Before she could answer, Glenn Odom spoke up. "I don't think we need a motion until we start talking about what we are sending to the Justice Department, which is the total response, including the elementary schools. I don't think you can separate the IB program from the total response."

I suppressed the urge to run screaming from the meeting. This was what I had hoped to avoid. We had been talking about elementary schools for nine months without agreement. I wanted to get agreement on the middle and high school plan so that we could make some progress. Glenn wanted a total package. I heard the call of the wild goose as we began the chase.

Glenn presented his proposal. "Let's accept the Justice Department plan with minor adjustments to some elementary school lines and include the NVEC plan. I know that many in the white community object to leaving North Vista all black, but they need to look at letting North Vista remain all black as a trade-off for not changing middle and high school lines. I strongly support the IB program."

For an hour board members reacted to Glenn's proposal. Carroll Player wanted to exclude the North Vista Education Committee plan. Doris Lockhart wanted the board to endorse the NVEC plan. Dick SoJourner and John Floyd didn't want to send the Justice Department anything. Randa Everett, attending her last meeting as a board member, worried about the advisability of leaving North Vista an all-black school.

At this point I was frustrated, thinking we had a solution before us but were unwilling to take it. We'd been on the merry-go-round so long, we had lost interest in the brass ring.

I tried to focus the group on the goal and the long-range impact of its decision. "I think about the early meetings, " I said. "On the first night, parents were expressing anger and frustrations. But at the second meeting a point came out that I haven't heard much of lately—that point being that whatever we do, we ought to solve this problem once and for all. We're doing right now what the district did twenty-three years ago. We have eight schools that can be called racially identifiable. If the IB program is implemented along with Plan Four [one of the board's plans for rezoning elementary schools], we only have one racially identifiable school left. If you look at the big picture, this has the possibility of resolving the issue.

"You can go to court. That's another way of getting it resolved, and you will get a final resolution. You'll spend a lot of time and you'll spend a lot of money, but I think you need to anticipate whether you would get a solution better than the one you can negotiate right now. We need to keep the big picture in mind."

Proud of myself after such a compelling argument, I anticipated board members would say, *he's right. Let's make the hard decision and solve this problem.* It didn't happen.

Since I didn't get the expected response, I turned to Laurence McIntosh and asked if a negotiated agreement with the Justice Department could become the basis for resolving the problem or would having a 100 percent black school preclude reaching a lasting solution. Laurence cooperated. "I don't see how the Justice Department could come before this school board recommending that North Vista be left alone and then on another day change their minds and do something else. Now some citizen may not like that school and decide to sue you at a later date. You can't prevent that."

Following Laurence's comments, several board members, especially Carroll Player and Doris Lockhart, continued to question and raise alternate solutions. Having allowed over an hour of free discussion, Anna Rose tried to get the board to address the issue, saying, "I think we need to decide if we're going to adopt a position to send to the Justice Department. The suggestions, as I understand them, are (1) to wait until Michael Maurer's visit and do nothing else, (2) to enhance Williams and Wilson with IB and enhance North Vista and leave other schools alone, (3) to do the same with Williams, Wilson, and North Vista and submit Plan Four, and (4) to do the same with Williams, Wilson, and North Vista, and submit Plan Six [an alternative plan for rezoning the elementary schools].

So I see there are four choices, four different opinions that we could submit. I frankly am ready to let the rubber meet the road. Let's decide on one of these things if we can. What do you want to do?"

John Floyd liked the option of doing nothing. "Let's vote to see if we want to do anything before Michael Maurer gets here."

Anna Rose said, "That needs to be a motion."

John said, "I make a motion that we not submit anything until after Michael Maurer visits and we see what direction he's going." Dick SoJourner seconded the motion.

We'd discussed the issue of submitting a plan to the Justice Department for over an hour, and the first motion was to do nothing. Before the vote I butted in again. "I need to give a little background. Michael Maurer is coming next Wednesday and Thursday and will be looking at schools. That's partly a result of my conversation with him, taking issue with his comments on facilities. He admitted not seeing the buildings. He requested something to look at and consider before he comes to move the negotiations along. It moves the timetable back if he doesn't have that. He would like to have something to look at."

Supporting me, Anna Rose said, "I specifically remember that suggestion. Do you, Mr. McIntosh?"

Laurence, who has been observing this spectacle with a bemused look on his face, supported my point, saying, "He, as a lawyer, needs to see the IB in advance, not to see it cold. If the IB program has no viability, there's no need to send it to Washington. If it does, and you are willing to discuss it, you would do well to let him see it in advance of coming here. There's no need to sandbag him. You don't have to adopt it tonight."

John Floyd tried another tactic and called on Larry Jackson, principal of Williams Middle School, who was sitting in the audience. "I don't think it's out of place to ask Mr. Jackson how he feels about the program and, from his conversations with him, how Mr. Brooks feels."

Larry said, "I would never speak for Mr. Brooks."

John wouldn't let it go. "You can speak from the conversations you've had with Mr. Brooks, not for him."

"I'd rather not do that. I am in favor of the IB program. I believe it will ultimately benefit all the students in the school."

John, who had made the motion to do nothing, said, "That's good enough for me to send a copy to Mr. Maurer in all due haste."

I squirmed in my seat. I had spent some time preparing a presentation on IB and had made a strong recommendation for it. I couldn't get board approval. Yet when a principal spoke one sentence in favor of the program, a board member reversed his position and supported the proposal. I knew I was losing influence with the board, but I hadn't realized it was that bad.

Calling on Laurence, Anna Rose said, "Mr. McIntosh, I understood you to say that we should submit the IB program, posthaste, to Washington, is that correct?"

Before Laurence could answer, Anna Rose cut him off. "Wait. I'm not done. I'll lose my train of thought if I don't finish. Are you suggesting that is the only thing we should send him right now?"

"I don't see the harm in sending him Plan Four if it has some viability with this board," Laurence answered. "It doesn't have to be a unanimous vote. It needs to have some viability."

Ready for a vote, Anna Rose asked, "Do you want to repeat your motion for clarification, Mr. Floyd?"

John said, "What? Oh, I think I know what it was. My motion was not to submit anything to Michael Maurer until after he has his visit."

When John's motion failed, Glenn moved to present a proposal to Michael Maurer that would include Plan Four, the NVEC plan, and the enhancement of Williams and Wilson, which would include at least the IB program.

After Miriam Baldwin seconded the motion, Carroll Player asked Glenn if he would accept an amendment that we retain the present middle and high school zones. Glenn accepted the amendment.

John Floyd, opposing the motion, said, "I'm opposed to sending him information that might jeopardize our negotiating position prior to the man coming. Because in his letter he referenced four incorrect statements in the five he made. I submit to you that the man doesn't know what is going on in Florence School District One, and I don't think we should send him proper knowledge of our district. Hopefully, you will educate him next week when he comes."

Glenn, defending his motion, responded. "Plan Four leaves only one school racially identifiable. Michael Maurer needs to understand this board is moving in the direction of eliminating racially identifiable schools. We need to get closure on this issue, closure that we have not had in twenty-three years. I think, as Dr. Player has said and I hope as I framed the motion, we're not locked into anything, but it shows the sentiment of this board."

Anna Rose agreed with Glenn. "That was my understanding of your motion, especially when you emphasized that we would present a proposed plan."

Carroll, thinking out loud, said, "If the board were to vote no on this amendment, I would think their thought process would be to present Michael Maurer with a plan leaving the other schools the same, and we would find out next week how he feels about that. Isn't that right, Laurence?"

Laurence answered, "I think you already know. You can have a racially identifiable school. You just have to justify it. There are four in Little Rock, Arkansas. The number of schools you have creates the burden. If you start with eight out of nineteen and get it down to one, then that becomes a workable thing. As you try to maintain more racially identifiable schools, each one adds to the burden of showing the justification."

Doris asked, "Dr. Player added an amendment to the motion to say there will be no zoning changes in the middle and high schools?"

Anna Rose replied, "Yes."

After Glenn's motion failed, Dick SoJourner offered a motion. "I'd like to present him a plan that we have discussed. To have the IB program as presented by Dr. Truitt, to leave North Vista as it is with the implementation of Dr. Reid's program at Dr. Reid's expense, and leave everything else alone."

John Floyd seconded Dick's motion, which failed.

I could see that everyone—with the possible exception of Doris—was enthusiastic about the IB program. It was the only thing we needed to send Maurer, but we couldn't get a vote to send it. I said, "Could we send IB only? No one has made that motion."

Randa supported my suggestion. "Let's go ahead and send the IB program," she said. "I'm obviously not going to be a part of it, but this group that's sitting right here is not of the same mind about what they want sent. Why not send just the IB program to Michael Maurer and give him time to digest that and know that there are two approaches for the elementary schools that the board is looking at and has not been able to resolve?"

"Can she add Dr. Reid's program at North Vista?" Carroll requested.

Incredible. Earlier in the meeting when Glenn included Dr. Reid's program, Carroll wanted it treated as a separate motion.

Miriam said what I was thinking. "I think this is ridiculous. We know what we've got to do."

Anna Rose repeated the motion, stating that the motion asks that we send all of our information on enhancement programs.

Glenn questioned her, "Are we sending a recommendation that the board is leaning toward those enhancements, including the NVEC plan? So you're saying you'd accept everything in my motion except Plan Four. Plan Four removes any racially identifiable schools except North Vista."

Miriam added, "And are we saying this is what we are proposing as a solution to racially identifiable schools? This is what this is all about, isn't it? This is what we are submitting as a solution, leaving everything else alone?"

Anna Rose, "I think Ms. Baldwin has a valid point. Is there any way that Michael Maurer can interpret what we are doing as addressing Williams and Wilson and that we don't intend to do anything else about the elementary schools?"

Miriam, "Exactly."

Frustrated, Randa cried, "Where is Larry Orr?"

Carroll answered, "He's smart. He's somewhere else."

Tired and discouraged, but determined to get the IB information to Michael Maurer, I said, "The thing that is concerning me is that I sense there is good support for the IB program. More than four people have made favorable, supportive comments of the IB program. Somehow, someway, we have to figure out a way of wording a motion so that I can send it to him. Would we have support for sending him the information on the IB program and saying the board is undecided on the elementary schools so that he could have the information? As Laurence said before, he doesn't have this information. Progress is hard to come by, and it could move us toward our goal if he at least had that."

Laurence added, "Do y'all have any objections if I send him this information, so he can do his homework?"

This drew laughter and a comment from Anna Rose, who said, "That sounds like a wonderful idea to me."

Dick SoJourner, now ready to go along, said, "I don't have any problem with sending it."

Doris, whose position on IB had not been established, said, "I appreciate Mr. Jackson raising the concerns I have with the IB program. In REACH [the program for academically talented elementary students], the percentages of black students we have in that program are minute, practically none. None of the parents addressed curriculums at those schools. They were concerned with how far their children were going to have to travel. If they had a concern about the curriculum, then they didn't say it. The Justice Department said we needed to enhance the curriculums at North Vista, Williams, and Wilson. However this board has said they don't have a problem: they are the same as any other school. So, to put the kind of money we're talking about into a IB program to my understanding is not going to encourage white parents to send their children there, based on what was said at the public hearings. They talked about being close to the schools."

Reacting to Doris, I said, "So what I hear you saying is that you are not opposed to the program; you're just not sure it will work."

"Right," Doris said.

I followed up. "If that's the case, it's still worth exploring. We can find out more about it as we explore. I proposed the IB program because I don't sense any support on this board for changing middle and high school attendance lines when there are alternatives that might work. This is one of the best approaches. I think it will work, and I think it will upgrade the academic level of our schools. So it seems to me as though it's something we should explore. I think we're down to the board saying go ahead and send it or letting Laurence send it."

Glenn, really frustrated now, says, "We are indeed splitting hairs. The IB program is great. School choice is great. Dr. Reid is great. What are we doing?"

Carroll Player had one more short speech. "I think the difference in this program and why it worked in Northeast and Spring Valley is that it is a volunteer program. And it changed the racial quotas without changing attendance lines. If it works, it's a very acceptable way of solving this problem. If this board's in favor of it, it ought to stand behind it and not tell Laurence to send it. We ought to send it. If that's all it takes, I'm gathering on the last vote it was Dr. Reid's program at North Vista that might have made it fail. I don't know why, but if we want to break it down to the IB program, I move that we forward the IB program to Michael Maurer."

After a two-hour meeting, the board approved Carroll's motion to submit the IB program for the middle and high schools to Michael Maurer, which was the action I had recommended in the first ten minutes of the meeting.

This meeting was typical of board meetings where the superintendent is unable to influence the board, which spends time and energy going off in different directions like foxes with their tails on fire. The meeting was atypical because the board enacted my recommendation as superintendent, but only after they had gone all over the map with their discussion.

On June 6, the day before Michael Maurer's visit to Florence, Denise Pridgen of the *Morning News* called, wanting to know his schedule. I referred her to Laurence McIntosh, who was arranging the visit. Since Laurence didn't return her call, Denise felt the district was putting a "veil" over the visit and wrote an article saying so when she missed the first day's visit. The article appeared on the front page. Maurer was incredulous that the paper would give such exposure to a nonstory. From my point of view, this type of sensationalism in reporting contributed to the tension in the community by creating the impression the board was not being open in its dealings.

At 10:30 on the morning of June 7, Maurer arrived at my office, bringing with him Dr. William Gordon, who had been a teacher and principal before attending law school at the University of South Carolina. Even though his business card listed his address as Dayton, Ohio, Gordon frequently mentioned his South Carolina roots.

When we sat down in my office, Laurence immediately seized the initiative and outlined the general terms of the board's position, gently confronting the visitors with a smile on his face. "You Washington gurus who live in your pristine, ivory towers inside the Beltway don't know what it's like to live in the real world. We live in the real world, and you need to understand that there are some things that we are not going to do. If you insist on doing those things, so be it. We'll fight you in court."

I jumped in. "Specifically, if you think we are going to change high school lines, then you may as well go back to Washington and prepare for court. This board will not change those lines."

We then talked about the IB program. Gordon, who was familiar with IB, supported the program as a magnet to attract white students to the Williams and Wilson schools. His main concern, which was echoed by Maurer, was how to enhance the program at North Vista. Always North Vista.

The Long,
TWENTY **Hot Summer**

We updated the board on the rezoning plan in July 1995. Even though the changes were minor, board members grumbled. After housing only grades K–4 for a couple of years, Royall Elementary School would again have fifth and sixth graders.

"We're going to have trouble with this change," Glenn Odom said. "Parents are going to be unhappy about not being able to send their children to Moore Intermediate School." When we had moved the fifth and sixth grades from Royal to Moore Intermediate to deal with overcrowding, Glenn and most other board members had thought parents would object. Now, under the leadership of Principal Debbie Cribb, Moore had become a parent favorite.

Porter Stewart asked, "How many portable classrooms do we have at McLaurin? Isn't this going to be our most difficult school to get parents to go to? What plans do we have to enhance McLaurin?"

John Floyd was upset by the way a neighborhood was divided between Royall, Delmae, and Briggs. "I don't think we're being fair to the people in these neighborhoods. I think we need to take another look at the plan," he said.

After I made it clear I was updating them on our negotiations and didn't expect them to vote, Anna Rose Rainwater said, "I'm sure this will be on our July agenda for action." I responded, "No. Our plan is to negotiate a package with the Justice Department and bring it to you for approval after we know we have something the Justice Department will accept."

At this point Laurence McIntosh came in, and the board moved to a discussion of the single-member district suit. Laurence told the board they had to come up with an alternative plan if they wanted the court to consider alternatives to single-member districts.

Anna Rose said, "I would like to see a plan for a board with six single-member districts with three at-large members drawn up for our review."

Glenn Odom lobbied for delay. "The U.S. Supreme Court is presently considering a case involving single-member districts. I think we need to wait until that case is decided. Besides, Larry Orr [who was absent] is interested in cumulative voting. We need to consider all the alternatives before hastily jumping into a single-member district plan of any kind."

During the discussion Laurence mentioned some information Carroll had asked him to prepare. Doris Lockhart interrupted and said, "Madam Chairman, what is he talking about? How did Dr. Player know what this meeting was about? Why wasn't I informed?"

Carroll Player responded. "Doris, everything we're talking about was in the memo that you received from Dr. Truitt."

After nearly twenty years as a superintendent, I knew the importance of communicating fairly with all board members. Because certain board members sought me out for additional information, it was difficult to maintain evenness in communication. For example, Dick SoJourner used to stop by my office several mornings a week just to chat. But I was meticulous in my communication with board members regarding board business.

In this case Doris had received the same information as other board members, but because of a lack of trust, she assumed I was sharing information with other board members to which she didn't have access. As the only African American on the board, Doris was in a tough position. She had no close allies on the board, and while I included her in my communication to the board, I am sure she was not included in informal discussions that took place between other members. Nor did she drop by my office for chats.

The board adjourned without taking any action, deciding to wait on the Supreme Court decision. It was following its familiar pattern of avoiding decisions until forced.

Later in July, Laurence McIntosh called to say that Michael Maurer of the Justice Department had concerns. Maurer alleged that North Vista didn't get the same level of maintenance as other schools. It would have been difficult to answer this charge earlier, but we had recently developed a detailed system recording maintenance work that showed North Vista submitted more work orders and had more work orders completed than any other elementary school. The school was third in the total amount spent and seventh in the per pupil amount spent on maintenance of the thirteen elementary schools.

Maurer also complained I had cut an assistant principal from the school last year, a concern that could only have come from Principal Clarence Alston. The extra assistant principal was a holdover from when North Vista was the largest elementary school in the district. Now, two schools with higher enrollments had the same level of staffing.

Maurer raised the issue of building a fence along the boundary of the new Carver School, a sore point with me. He had suggested this during lunch on an earlier visit. I nearly jumped across the table at PA's Restaurant to tell him he had a legitimate right to talk with us about racial balance in the schools, but we would decide where to put fences. The Concerned Citizens for Excellence in Education, anxious about a rundown joint located on the west boundary of the proposed school, had raised the fence issue. The joint looked like an old motel and was probably a house of prostitution, but since it operated only on weekends, I didn't see it as a threat.

Listening to Laurence enumerate Maurer's concerns, I realized Maurer was getting his information from the North Vista Education Committee and the Concerned Citizens for Excellence in Education. I responded to each concern, rejecting most of them. Laurence was not happy, wanting me to be more conciliatory.

The next day we got a request from the NAACP lawyers for interrogatories and production of documents for the single-member district suit. The plaintiff wanted copies of every teacher's contract from 1971 through 1995 (850 teachers times 15 years = 12,750 contracts), a list of every student who had been suspended for the same time period, a list of students in gifted and special education classes for the same time period, and on and on and on—forty-six interrogatories in all.

My staff and I met with Laurence to discuss the data collection. Even though Rick Reames said it was the "biggest bunch of crap he'd ever seen," my staff agreed we could collect most of the information. None of us believed the requested data had anything to do with single-member districts, but Laurence wanted to provide the information to accomplish two purposes—to show the judge we were cooperative and not hiding anything and to give the NAACP lawyers a mound of useless information to study.

Early in the summer, I accepted an invitation to speak at a meeting of the Northwest Community Council, the group that represented the Carver School neighborhood. Located a couple of blocks from Carver Elementary School, the Northwest Community Council's building was a depressing, windowless, one-story cinder-block building with a solid metal door. *Nothing light and cheery about this place*, I thought when I arrived at 6:55 P.M.

Teachers at Carver didn't feel safe in this neighborhood. They said drug dealing was rampant. Already uneasy about the meeting, I grew more apprehensive when I found the building locked and no one around. My blood pressure went up a few points when Denise Pridgen of the *Florence Morning News* pulled up beside me. I had not considered the press would attend a neighborhood meeting.

At 7:00 a lady showed up and opened the building. Counting the reporter and me, seven people were assembled. Nevertheless, Jimmy Harrison, who chaired the Northwest Community Council, started the meeting on time.

Since I understood that year-round schools were an issue, I began by explaining about the year-round program at Royall. A woman in the audience interrupted and asked how another school could get the program. I explained that the Royall principal and faculty initiated the program and that other schools could do the same. Once this question was asked, my presentation was cut off. The meeting became a question and answer session.

Most questions were about the location of the Carver School. I defended the selection of the Sumter/Cashua site and told them we were moving ahead with the project and would advertise for bids in the coming week. Not understanding the significance of the bidding process, several people asked for reconsideration of the location. One lady repeated the rumor that the board had promised some black ministers that they would leave the school in the community.

Denise Pridgen left at 7:30 to write her article, which appeared the next morning, outlining the community dissatisfaction with the school board and superintendent. Had she stayed longer, Denise would have had more material for her article. As the meeting dragged on and on, lasting until 9:00, the criticism escalated and became sharper.

Throughout the summer Laurence had negotiated with the Justice Department. When they accepted the proposal to put the IB program at the middle and high schools, North Vista was the only remaining hurdle in the negotiations.

I wasn't happy with the Justice Department's emphasis on North Vista because the school already received more Title I money ($450,000) than any other school. Even so, enhancing North Vista would cost less than a court battle with the Justice Department. To develop a proposal for enhancing North Vista, I talked with Principal Clarence Alston. Clarence wanted a technology specialist and a couple of hundred thousand dollars worth of building improvements.

In late July I presented these proposals for enhancing North Vista to the board. The majority seemed willing to make accommodations for the school, but they opted to hold another meeting before making a decision.

With the North Vista enhancements still unresolved, Clarence Alston asked to appear before the board at the September meeting. He said, "North Vista has received a lot of bad publicity in the rezoning discussions. I'd like to give the board a more positive picture." On the morning of the meeting, I met with him to review his presentation. He didn't have much written down, and I encouraged him to get into the specifics. He said that he would and that he would put it in writing.

I wanted Alston to give a "We've Been Making Progress at North Vista, and Here's Some Things We're Going to Do to Get Better This Year" speech. Instead, he gave a "We've Been Making Progress at North Vista, but We're Handicapped by the Board's Lack of Endorsement of the North Vista Education Committee Plan, and I Want You to Endorse It" speech. The board in the past had expressed general approval of his plan but had requested specifics. Again they asked for specifics, but Alston didn't give any. The next morning Denise Pridgen's article said that Alston had asked for board support and had been put on hold.

While the *Florence Morning News* promoted controversy, WBTW-TV, Channel 13, under the leadership of Lou Kirchen, the general manager, proved to be a friend of the school district. Lou agreed to serve as a consultant for our district marketing team and to develop a video to hold and build public support for rezoning changes. She also made her creative and production staffs available to the school district.

In mid-September board chair Anna Rose Rainwater called to say that Doris Lockhart had told her that the Northwest Community Council was unhappy with Carver principal Cynthia Young. Community members complained that Cynthia did not give feedback to parents, hired primarily white teachers (seven of eight), and referred to the staff as "you people," a Ross Perot–like term that black staff found offensive.

After Anna Rose's call, I called Cynthia and learned that Larry McCutcheon had called her about the same issues. She had planned a meeting with him and some other ministers.

Immediately after my conversation with Cynthia, I got a call from Calvin Thomas requesting that Cynthia, Sara Slack, and I meet with the Northwest Community Council and Carver parents on October 2. I agreed to the meeting, and when I learned that rezoning was an issue, I asked Rick Reames to join us.

Having been ambushed by the media at a Northwest Community meeting earlier in the summer, I asked Calvin not to invite the media. On the day of the meeting, the *Florence Morning News* carried an announcement of the meeting. Calvin called and apologized, disavowing responsibility for the announcement.

Once again I returned to the Northwest Community Center building. Inside, a table and three metal chairs faced six rows of chairs divided into two sections by an aisle. Since all the chairs were full, people stood leaning against the walls and sat on tables. A sign on the wall proclaimed it was unsafe for more than ninety persons to occupy the building. I judged there were more than ninety present, and I did not feel safe.

Jimmy Harrison, chair of the Northwest Community Council and a stroke victim, spoke slowly, slurring his words, but he started the meeting on time. I called on Rick Reames to deal with the first topic on the agenda—rezoning.

Even though the rezoning plan had been publicized and I had talked about it at my earlier meeting with the Northwest Community Council, most people didn't know where their children would be going to school under this plan. As Rick passed out maps, the audience mumbled and grumbled. Calvin rapped his pencil on the table, calling for order whenever the crowd noise drowned out the speaker. Many had difficulty understanding the maps, and Rick went over them repeatedly. Each time a question was asked, the crowd murmured. A few asked questions. Some made speeches about how unfair the plan was.

The group did not accept that the Justice Department was ordering rezoning —even though the Northwest Community Council leaders had claimed credit for calling the Justice Department to Florence. We were accused of lying about where we were going to build the school and of planning to put white kids in the new school and send black kids to an older one.

We had discussed rezoning plans in open meetings for a year. These meetings were front-page news in the local press, yet this group seemed unaware that the meetings had been held.

In publicizing the public meetings, we had made a gross mistake, depending on the newspaper articles to inform the community. Most of the Carver community had not followed the well-publicized meetings. Now as we seemed to be presenting these plans as a fait accompli, these citizens felt as though the locomotive was running over them without blowing its whistle.

As the meetings dragged on, Calvin tried to shift to other topics. The crowd turned on him, saying the NAACP didn't do anything but put things off. As the session deteriorated into a series of accusations, Calvin moved on, calling on Cynthia Young.

Cynthia answered questions about discipline, truancy, teacher motivation, and various other topics about Carver School. The crowd responded with hostility and accusations to her comments about the number of retentions. Some parents raised issues involving their own children, matters that could not be discussed without violating privacy rights.

Calvin had promised the meeting would last no more than an hour. We were still going at 8:15 and moving to a third topic, the firing of a former cafeteria manager at Carver, who was in the room. I refused to discuss a personnel matter in a public meeting. Calvin, citing his experience on the school board, supported me.

Someone asked why we didn't hire more black teachers. I pointed out that we had offered contracts to thirty-four of forty-one black candidates and to only 30 percent of the white candidates the previous year. I also told the crowd that we employed a district recruiter, who was black, and that we were members of the Pee Dee Minority Recruitment Center.

Elder James Williams challenged me, saying, "We've had two generations of integrated schools. You can't tell me there aren't enough black teachers out there. Besides, I know several black teachers who've applied to Florence School District One and have not been hired."

I responded, "We do not hire every black who applies. We look for the best people."

The crowd swelled as additional people drifted in during the meeting. City councilman Ed Robinson, who had not been present when the meeting started, made a speech. Robinson told the crowd they could see for themselves the bias and racial injustice he was fighting on city council, saying it was just like slavery in 1849. He told them they needed a "retaliatory plan."

I was sitting there, my head spinning, wondering what would happen next, as the meeting went on and on. At 9:00 I whispered to Calvin that we ought to end it, and he did, promising the crowd a follow-up meeting. The headlines the next morning read, "District One Officials Blasted by Residents."

Negotiations with the Justice Department dragged on into September. Michael Maurer was hung up on getting an additional assistant principal for North Vista. I refused to budge on this issue.

In mid-October, Laurence called to tell me that Maurer had dropped his demand for the North Vista assistant principal although he had other demands: an additional day for the part-time teacher of gifted and talented at North Vista, a local commitment for computers, and connections to the Internet for the school. Even though I told Laurence I would not agree to new demands, he said we should go to the board with our proposal, believing Maurer was just pushing our buttons. Laurence recommended we get board approval on an agreement and present it to Maurer, telling him he could take it or leave it.

Before meeting with the board, Laurence and I met with managing editor Frank Sayles and publisher Tom Marschel of the *Florence Morning News* to explain the proposed agreement to them.

Later in the afternoon, we met with the board. Although we had announced the board would be meeting in executive session, we decided to meet openly. About thirty people sat in the audience as Laurence went over the proposed fourteen-page agreement almost word-by-word, taking about thirty minutes.

When Chair Rainwater asked for questions, Carroll Player spoke up, "We haven't given in to all the Justice Department demands, have we?"

Doris Lockhart asked, "What are we doing for North Vista? Is this school getting the enhancements needed to bring it up to par?"

Dick SoJourner said, "I'm all for settling this matter, but I want it settled for good. If we agree to this, is the Justice Department going to come back on us some other time in the future?"

During this question period, Glenn Odom passed Anna Rose a note reminding her that he needed to be at church by 6:30. Miriam Baldwin had previously told Anna Rose that she also had to leave at a certain time. Anna Rose wrote Glenn a note telling him to make a motion. He moved that the board authorize Laurence and me to sign an agreement with the Justice Department on behalf of the board. The motion passed unanimously.

The plan approved by the board rezoned all the elementary schools except North Vista and required 41 percent of our elementary students to change schools. Attendance lines for the middle and high schools remained the same with a commitment to implement the IB program at Williams Middle School and Wilson High School.

Implementing the Plan

TWENTY-ONE

While the negotiated agreement with the Justice Department had resolved the district's legal complaints, the community's mood was uglier than a wounded mama bear. We had less than a year to convince the public to support the new school assignments.

The pressures of so many controversial issues were taking their toll on me. I couldn't sleep, getting up at all hours of the night to work on district business. On December 7, 1995, I got up at 4:00 A.M. and wrote a newspaper article, a letter, and my weekly memo to the board. When I went to office at 7:30, I met with board chair Anna Rose Rainwater to discuss a couple of sensitive issues.

One issue involved Elder James Williams, who claimed to have been disrespected at South Florence High School by Pat Magee, an assistant principal. Williams complained to the board that I hadn't gotten back to him about his grievance. Williams's original complaint stemmed from an incident at South Florence High School. According to Williams, he was not treated with respect by the school administration when he complained about his son's suspension.

Magee told a different version of the incident. According to Ms. Magee, the controversy began when Williams's son refused to take his assigned seat on the bus when asked by the bus driver, the bus supervisor, and another assistant principal. For this refusal, Magee had suspended young Williams for three days. Later that same day, Elder Williams came to the school, unannounced, to argue the suspension. Magee listened to him and then passed him off to William Hamilton, another assistant principal, who spent two hours with Williams.

When Williams came back to Magee's office, nearly three hours after his arrival, she told him she couldn't help him anymore. When he refused to leave her office, she did. Magee went to Principal Curt Boswell and told him what had happened. Boswell left Williams cooling his heels in Magee's office.

Williams went to the district office after he tired of waiting. I was out, and Jerry Wilkes, my secretary, spent an hour with him, calling the school, pulling up the boy's attendance and discipline record on the computer, showing Williams that the boy was not going to lose credit over this suspension. When she told him she would share his complaint with me, she thought the matter had been resolved. But now Williams was complaining to the board about lack of follow-through.

After explaining this background to Anna Rose, we agreed she would send Williams a letter apologizing for his being "disrespected" and suggest he make appointments when he had business at the school. I didn't think this response would satisfy Williams and expected him to show up at the board meeting the following week, which was shaping up to be a doozy.

A letter, "Notice to Carver Parents," was being passed out at churches in the Carver community, inviting parents to attend the December board meeting, saying,

> If you are a parent of a child now attending Carver School, you are required to meet with the Florence School Board at the monthly meeting at the district office on Thursday, the 14th of December, 1995, at 7:00 P.M.
>
> At this meeting you will express objections to having your child bussed away from his or her own neighborhood to make space for rich white children who will become the new occupants of the new state of the arts school.
>
> You must object to your children being treated like little dirt bags who are not decent enough to attend school with rich kids from Windsor Forest and Whitehall.
>
> You will make it clear that the lines have been drawn improperly and with malice aforethought in the continual effort by the superintendent and the school board to continue their concerted efforts to deny a proper education to black kids.
>
> If these concerns are yours, the Northwest Community Council will meet you at the next meeting of the school board.

As an educator, I was perplexed that anyone would think a school board and its superintendent would engage in a concerted effort to deny a proper education to black kids. No doubt this had been done in earlier years, but at this juncture, boards and superintendents were concentrating on raising the test scores of all children. The achievement gap between white and black students was being acknowledged and addressed.

When I had come to Florence, the district had pre-first classes, which amounted to a second year of kindergarten. Blacks were overrepresented in these classes, meaning many were a year older than their peers in first grade. I had eliminated these classes and implemented a Reading Recovery program, which was designed to allow first-grade students having trouble with reading to catch up without being retained. This change, resisted by some principals, had not been easy to make, but I had pushed because I thought it was the right thing to do. It hurt that now I was being accused of not caring about the education of black children.

By 7:00 P.M., when the meeting was scheduled to begin, only James Williams and Judith Poston had signed up to speak. Poston, the head of the local teachers' association who only spoke on teacher benefit issues, was not there to speak about Carver. After the meeting started, other people drifted in until about twenty were present. Of the twenty, only three were parents affected by rezoning. The others were older people from the community who did not have children in the school.

Even though he lived in Effingham, at least ten miles from the controversial elementary school, James Williams assumed the role of spokesman for the North Vista community. He attacked the board, accusing them of accommodating rich white kids at the expense of black students. He called for a change in leadership. In closing, he asked for information on the rumor that the Carver faculty would not "facilitate" the new school but would be replaced.

Since board policy prohibited response to public participation at the meeting, Anna Rose thanked Williams for his presentation and continued with the meeting. Most of the Carver crowd remained at the meeting for a while, leaving only after they realized that the board wasn't going to respond to Williams.

The morning newspaper headlines read, "Neighborhood Council Calls for Board's Resignation." The article made it clear that my resignation was a part of the requested leadership change.

Because of the winter break, the January board meeting seemed to come quickly after the December one. Elder Williams was back, this time asking for my resignation because the African American community didn't like my leadership. To support his request, Williams cited the low percentage of black teachers in the district. He also mentioned that I had neither responded to his complaint about Pat Magee nor taken appropriate action. He would have said more, but Anna Rose cut him off after the five-minute time limit.

The next morning the newspaper quoted Williams as emphasizing they were not asking for my resignation but for the board to replace me with someone who "would provide unbiased and fair representation of all the parents in the district." He added that his request was in part motivated by the expulsion of "an A student with no history of discipline problems."

The expulsion he referred to was that of a Southside student whose hearing had been before the board the previous week. His mother, who was a preacher, and a local lawyer represented the student. The boy had brought a knife to school for protection and had given it to a girl to keep for him. The mother and the lawyer seemed to think the boy was justified in bringing a knife to school since he felt threatened. The board expelled the boy by a vote of 7–1, with Doris Lockhart voting against the expulsion. Since the student's right to privacy prevented me from putting the facts of the expulsion before the public, Williams's version of it went unchallenged in the public meeting.

The next day Tommy Cooper, director of secondary education and a black man, came by and told me he thought I had taken a cheap shot the previous night, referring to Williams's call for my resignation. While Tommy was in my office, Larry Jackson, the principal of Williams Middle School, called and joked that he was not present when African Americans voted on my leadership. Anna Rose and several other people also called, wanting to know if I was all right.

I was, but I didn't like the situation. I didn't want to be controversial or to become an issue in the spring school board elections.

Near the end of January, we sent out seven thousand letters to parents of elementary students, notifying them of school assignments for the coming year. In spite of extensive publicity about rezoning, most parents hadn't realized how they would be affected until they received those letters. Dozens called our office. We put in an answering machine so parents could call after hours, leave their questions, and get an answer later. Rick Reames asked me to listen to one of the callers on the answering machine. The lady, who identified herself as a mother of a Dewey Carter Elementary School student who was being transferred to Savannah Grove, let us know our plan was "stoopid, stoopid, stoopid."

Late one afternoon I got a call from a man who was upset his son was being transferred from Delmae to Royall. He had called Governor Beasley and, if you believe him, had talked with the governor. He had also called Senators Strom Thurmond and Ernest Hollings, the Justice Department, and Congressman James Clyburn. This man couldn't understand why the people didn't get to vote on this issue. He said he was going to come to our next board meeting and fight as hard as he could to prevent this change. I never heard from him again.

At the end of this busy January in which Elder Williams had demanded the board fire me, I had my evaluation. The board meeting was scheduled for 5:30 P.M. At 4:00 Wayne Fournier, a reporter from WPDE-TV, Channel 15, called. "Dr. Truitt," he began, "I was wondering if you would go on camera this afternoon and discuss the board meeting to evaluate you?"

I declined, saying, "Wayne, it would be improper for me to discuss my evaluation. That's the board's business. If you want a quote on my evaluation, you need to contact Anna Rose Rainwater, who chairs the board."

Wayne was not anything if not persistent. He said, "I'm coming to the school board office at 5:15. Will you be in the building?"

"I will be in the building, but I am not commenting on my evaluation."

Wayne did not show up before the meeting. At 5:30 the board went into executive session, and I went back to my office. Each year the board evaluated me, and I had never had a bad evaluation. Still, I hated sitting alone in my office waiting, not knowing how the discussion was going. As time dragged on, wild and crazy thoughts raced through my mind. By 6:25, when the board called me to the boardroom, I had convinced myself that the board was going to fire me and that I would be better off if they did.

When I walked across to the boardroom, Wayne was interviewing Anna Rose in the lobby. As I walked by, I heard enough to understand that Wayne was trying to connect this evaluation, which was an annual process, with Elder Williams's call for my resignation.

The feedback session with the board went well. I received compliments on each of the areas on which I was evaluated, as well as suggestions for improvement. Anna Rose encouraged me to interrupt at any time, but I said little in the twenty-five-minute session. At the end of the session, they voted 8–0 to extend my contract for another year. Without doubt, Elder Williams, by calling for my resignation, had helped me, prodding the board to act on my evaluation. I was relieved and encouraged to receive a vote of confidence.

Trying to ease concerns about the new zoning plan and wanting to promote its acceptance, each elementary school held a question-and-answer session for parents in the spring. About sixty parents showed up for the first one at Delmae Elementary School. Principal Addie Cain presented information about the school and then fielded questions. I was pleased that parents asked for information, rather than making emotional statements. The meeting lasted only forty minutes.

I worried about McLaurin School. The rezoning plan required children from the Cloisters, one of Florence's most exclusive neighborhoods, to transfer from Briggs to McLaurin. I wasn't sure these parents would send their children to McLaurin since they could afford private schools.

McLaurin's location was a major problem. Isolated at the end of a dead-end road in a run-down section of Florence, literally on the other side of the tracks, the school was hard to get to. Parents had to time their morning school delivery carefully to avoid a long train that stopped in Florence, blocking the tracks and cutting off the route to McLaurin. Besides its location, McLaurin had image problems. Approximately 90 percent of the school's students were black, and the school served as a center for the special education program, housing several classes for mentally handicapped students.

To make McLaurin more appealing, I was transferring Martin Smith, the longtime principal at Briggs to McLaurin. In February 1996 I was encouraged to see that parents packed the school cafetorium for the question-and-answer session.

Rebecca Smith, the current McLaurin principal, and Martin had jointly planned the meeting. Rebecca opened the program by having a four-year-old boy sing a song. He was cute, but I didn't understand the point of having him sing. Parents had come to find out about the school. Rebecca then told them the history of McLaurin School. After about twenty-five minutes, she turned the program over to Martin.

Martin is not a polished speaker. He stutters slightly, but he exudes sincerity. The audience, which was about 85 percent Briggs parents, hung on to his every word. After watching the parents' reaction to Martin, I slept better that night, thinking this thing may work.

In February 1996 six people signed up to speak to the board. I detested public participation at our board meetings. Most presentations should not have come to the board. They could have been handled by the administration. Many of the speakers who appeared before the board seemed to be seeking publicity, rather than a solution to their concerns. This meeting was no exception.

Elder Williams was back, having spoken at five or six previous meetings. Williams began by saying he was considering a defamation of character suit against board member Miriam Baldwin because she had been quoted in the paper as saying he had tried to get the board involved in a shouting match. He then renewed his attack on me, saying, "Just because you renewed the superintendent's contract, don't think the matter is over. It's not." He concluded by accusing the board of ignoring the black community.

Several white parents followed Williams, complaining about rezoning and the babysitting and transportation problems caused by the new attendance lines.

A father whose son had been suspended from West Florence High School for smoking marijuana wanted to know if his son would be eligible to play baseball if he moved into the Wilson area.

A mother wanted the board to extend the exam exemption to middle school students who take high school courses.

Charles Foxe, a regular public participant, had a list of concerns. He asked the board to schedule a series of special meetings to engage in dialogue with the black community.

After Foxe, the board had to deal with the follow-up of a previous appearance by Teresa Ervin, who wanted the board to consider adjusting the rezoning plan to bring more of the current Carver School students back into the new Carver zone. Board chair Anna Rose Rainwater and I had met earlier with Mrs. Ervin and Northwest community leaders Harriet Smith and Roy Cunningham. In a conciliatory mood, Anna Rose asked them to identify streets to be rezoned and let her know.

Now Anna Rose presented this request to the board and got no support from her fellow members. I was glad the board didn't make any adjustments, but I worried that the Northwest community leaders would feel they had been given false hope.

Justice Department Hearing

TWENTY-TWO

I went into education because I wanted to teach history and coach basketball. After three years of full-time teaching, the principal at the junior high school where I taught asked me to be assistant principal. From that point on, I moved up the administrative ladder, becoming superintendent in Danville, Virginia, at age thirty-five. On March 7, 1996, facing a public hearing on our agreement with the Justice Department, I felt I had made a wrong turn on my career path. This was not why I had become an educator.

The previous night we held a public hearing at Poynor Adult Education Center to allow people who wanted to address the court the next day to sign up. The meeting should have lasted ten minutes. It lasted two hours.

In the early stages of developing a racial balance plan, we had invited NAACP representatives to a meeting to ask for their suggestions for integrating the schools. At that time they said they would go along with whatever the Justice Department proposed. Now they were complaining to the Justice Department.

Anna Rose, who was presiding, sat on the platform with board attorney Laurence McIntosh, Justice Department attorneys Michael Maurer and Nick Brustin, Rick Reames, and me. Most of the questions were directed to the lawyers.

African American leaders questioned leaving North Vista all black. They wanted white students bused to North Vista and were insulted that it was not happening. Speaker after speaker harped on this issue, taking the Justice Department to task for permitting it.

Blacks from the Carver neighborhood were upset because some of them were being bused to Delmae. They felt they were being punished for contacting the Justice Department.

The board and I were called racists directly and indirectly. Franklin Briggs asked why the board wouldn't fire me.

Michael Maurer was cool under fire, defending the plan, refusing to accept fallacious premises in questions. He projected a tough confidence and was thorough in his answers.

The next morning when the lawyers met in my office, the agreement almost fell apart. We planned to finance the enhancements to North Vista with Title I funds to avoid increasing local taxes. Laurence McIntosh had maintained that the source of the funding didn't make any difference as long as we made the enhancements, but he had never discussed this with the Justice Department attorneys. Someone, the night before, had informed Maurer of our funding plans, and he hit the ceiling.

I refused to back down. "This is the only way we can finance the enhancements to North Vista. We do not have the local resources required," I insisted.

Laurence added, "If you want it done differently, then you need to bring your checkbook."

When we got to the courtroom, Maurer called Laurence aside and fussed some more. Laurence told me later that Maurer was close to calling off the whole deal.

The hearing was in the main courtroom of the McMillan Federal Building in downtown Florence. After getting off the elevator and passing through metal detectors, we entered the courtroom. The judge sat on an elevated platform at the back of the room, literally looking down on everyone. A stenographer and a clerk sat just below him. The lawyers' tables were well back from the bench, creating an empty space about the size of a volleyball court.

The Justice Department attorneys sat on the right; Laurence McIntosh, Rick Reames, and I sat at a large table on the left. The board members were not required to attend, but several did. Anna Rose Rainwater, Larry Orr, Doris Lockhart, Carroll Player, and John Floyd sat in chairs just behind us. On the wall to my left was a large clock, whose ticking in quiet moments reminded me of the clock in *High Noon*, counting down to the big showdown.

Stocky, graying, wearing half-glasses, Michael Duffy, the federal judge from Charleston, profusely thanked everyone for coming and commended the district and the Justice Department for holding a public hearing.

Michael Maurer opened the hearing with a fifty-minute statement. Laurence's five-minute opening emphasized we were agreeing to the consent order without admitting any deficiencies.

Maurer then called his only witness, Kelly Carey, an engineer/lawyer/school-zoning expert. Until this court appearance, I had not been impressed with Carey. Now I revised my opinion as he flawlessly answered Maurer's questions for thirty minutes. His assertion that North Vista could not be integrated without causing great problems was the bedrock of the agreement. He also argued that the original site for Carver was inappropriate.

Immediately after Carey finished, I took the stand as the first witness for the school district. For thirty minutes I answered Laurence's questions, finishing at 12:10. The Justice Department lawyers requested a recess before beginning the cross-examination, and after a ten-minute break, I took the stand again. Nick Brustin began the questioning, forcing me to say we would honor the agreement on North Vista, regardless of funding, asking me about Title I funding for the present project. He then took me through the entire consent order and had me commit to everything in it. I had the feeling he would enjoy putting me in jail if I failed to meet any of those commitments.

I finished at 12:50. Rick Reames followed me to the stand and was questioned by Laurence for ten minutes. The Justice Department lawyers did not cross-examine him. Laurence then put Anna Rose Rainwater on for five minutes, ending the testimony phase of the hearing.

Apologizing for the lateness of the hour, Judge Duffy said the public hearing would start in fifteen minutes, at 1:20. There would be no lunch break. Beginning the hearing, Judge Duffy announced he was going to give everyone who had signed up—all thirty-eight—ten minutes each to speak, even if we had to stay until 8:00.

The first speaker, Dr. John Bruce, who lived within walking distance of Royall and was being rezoned to Briggs, complained that his children would have to ride a bus to school out of his neighborhood.

Lucy Davis, a former school board member, was the second speaker. She sounded her favorite theme, doing what's best for children.

After a couple of low-key speakers, a quartet of passionate black speakers followed. Mrs. June Smith shed tears about North Vista remaining all black. Elder James Williams presented the judge with a copy of the North Vista Education Committee plan. Charles Foxe was the first speaker to have time called on him. Teresa Ervin pleaded to allow current Carver students to go to the new Carver.

A retired white teacher from Massachusetts spoke of her experience in volunteering at North Vista and being told by a student that he hates all white people.

Black county councilman Terry Alexander was calmer and didn't call us names. Dr. Roy Cunningham referred to North Vista as a "segregated prison." He believed the Carver community was being punished for calling the Justice Department.

After a series of black speakers sounded familiar themes, Nancy Rawl, a white mother of middle and high school students, encouraged the judge to sign the consent order—the only speaker to favor the order.

Former state senator Frank Gilbert spoke in his usual rambling style. The highlight of his presentation was a story about white Timrod Elementary School teachers getting upset over a black teacher telling students that blacks controlled the General Assembly after the Civil War. He spoke for thirteen minutes and was the only speaker allowed to go over the ten-minute limit.

Jimmy Harrison, chair of the Northwest Community Council, said we were not telling the truth. Back in the summer Mr. Harrison had asked me about building sidewalks for the new Carver School. I told him the board didn't build sidewalks. At the hearing on the previous night, he had asked Anna Rose Rainwater the same question, and she said the board would do everything possible for the safety of the students, creating the impression we would build sidewalks. Mr. Harrison said somebody was lying.

Ex–school board chair Calvin Thomas, the final speaker, warned the judge that if he signed the order, the NAACP would be back before him or some other judge. According to Calvin, this is "not a threat but a promise."

The public hearing was over at 3:45. Laurence had been taking thorough notes during the hearing, leading me to expect that the lawyers would be allowed to respond to the public comments. Not so. The judge thanked everyone for coming and adjourned, asking to see the lawyers in his chambers. Since I had ridden over with Laurence, I caught a ride back to the office with Larry Orr.

Back at the office, I bought a pack of cheese crackers for my lunch and reflected on the day. I didn't like being a superintendent anymore. After thirty years in education, twenty-one as a superintendent, I was ticked off and distressed at being called a liar and a racist.

Laurence, wound as tight as a golf ball, called at 5:00 to report on the meeting in chambers. The judge had raised questions about North Vista remaining all black, but Michael Maurer strongly defended the arrangement. Laurence believed the judge would sign the order, probably within two weeks.

The next morning the *Florence Morning News* headlines read, "Zoning Foes Address Judge: Tales of Racism, Lies, and Deceit Conveyed at Public Hearing." The entire article focused on the public hearing, providing no report on the evidentiary part of the proceedings. A second article included comments from Laurence McIntosh, who speculated that the judge would rule shortly and send his opinion to the district in writing.

A week after the hearing, I was preparing for the March board meeting when my secretary came in and said, "We're having a demonstration outside."

"We're having a what?"

"It's a demonstration. Some people from North Vista and Carver are picketing outside," she said.

I hated board meetings anyway. I didn't want to have to deal with a demonstration. I felt sick to my stomach, but I didn't go to the window to look. I stayed in my office and hoped the demonstration would not prevent board members from attending the meeting.

The demonstration had started late in the afternoon and was timed to get exposure on the 6:00 news. They did get some television coverage, but I wouldn't have known we were having a demonstration if I hadn't been told. The demonstrators stayed in the parking lot, and those of us inside didn't realize what was going on.

Once again we had a lengthy public participation session, with most of the participants being parents whose children were rezoned from Royall. These parents wanted their children to be allowed to stay at the school to participate in the year-round program.

The next day the newspaper gave front-page coverage to the demonstration. Anna Rose called and told me the news anchor at Channel 13 said the protest set off a "near riot." When Anna Rose called the station, the reporter said she probably shouldn't have said that and referred Anna Rose to her producer who also apologized. I called Lou Kirchen, the general manager of the station, and registered my complaint.

During these tough times I received encouragement and support from many people. Tom Kinard hosted a three-hour morning show on the radio that mixed community information with music. Every week I went on Tom's show to report on school district happenings. The day after the demonstrations, Tom, off the air, said I was always welcome and lit into the demonstrators.

At a staff breakfast Jane Ames, an adult education teacher, hugged me and told me I was a wonderful superintendent. Later in the day Bryan Jackson, president of Superior Machine Company, called. Bryan, who was dying of cancer, told me if I needed any "counterinsurgency action," just to let him know. He said he was going to call school board members and convey his support for me.

When you're at the center of controversy, it's easy to think the whole world is against you. I appreciated the support of Tom, Jane, Bryan, and others who let me know I still had some friends and supporters.

In early June, Judge Duffy issued his ruling implementing the plan. This time the *Florence Morning News* supported the school district, writing an editorial critical of Calvin Thomas and Billy Isgett for refusing to accept the decision, pointing out that it was time to move forward.

Teacher Dismissal

Two weeks after the Justice Department hearing, first-year Lester Elementary School principal Marlene Williams and I met with a Lester teacher to tell her I was recommending her dismissal. I hated firing people and was always tense confronting a person, even when I had solid evidence for the action, as I did in this case.

This teacher was a single mother and a hard worker. She volunteered for extra assignments at school but still found time to be an active parent. During the time I had known her, she had served as PTA president at two different schools. But she had a problem. Fourteen of fifteen children in the teacher's class had reported that the teacher had pinched or manhandled them. Parents were requesting that their children be removed from her classroom. The teacher already was on probation for similar problems in the past.

In spite of the evidence against her, the teacher denied hitting the children. Ignoring her denial, I asked, "Do you have a problem that you need help with?"

"No," she said.

I continued, "We have a serious problem here." Surprised that she came to the conference alone, I added, "You may want representation. Since you are facing a possible dismissal, you may want to consider contacting the South Carolina Education Association."

"I didn't join this year. I couldn't afford it."

At this point Marlene interrupted and asked, "Dr. Truitt, would you let her resign?"

To suggest resignation weakens the case against dismissal, and I would have not brought it up. But after Marlene, in a sincere effort to help the teacher, introduced the idea, I said, "Yes."

The teacher, who had remained calm and unemotional throughout the conference said, "I'll need some time to think about it."

The teacher did not resign. She decided to get a lawyer and fight her dismissal.

On the day of her hearing, April 18, her attorney, Steve Wukela, called and wanted to deal—a job teaching smaller groups rather than a full class. I rebuffed his offer but countered with an offer to keep her on the payroll for the remainder of the year in return for her immediate resignation. I then called Laurence McIntosh and told him of my conversation. Laurence called Wukela and continued to negotiate.

Wukela wanted three things: her salary for the remainder of the year, neutral recommendations for references, and that her files be purged of negative materials. I balked at the third request. Laurence then worked out a compromise—place the negative evaluations and letters in an envelope, available only to district personnel. I agreed and thought we had a deal.

Nothing happened. About 4:00, just ninety minutes before the hearing was to begin, I called Laurence. He told me the teacher was on her way to Wukela's office to sign the agreement.

Time passed. Still no word. At 5:15 Wukela walked into my office and said he was looking for his client. She hadn't shown up at his office. Wukela, a big man with a salt and pepper beard, usually had a smile on his cherubic face, but today he wasn't smiling.

When his client arrived at 5:30, Wukela met with her privately. He came back in five minutes and said she wanted to go through with the hearing. He didn't say anything else, but his head shaking and eye rolling told me his client was not following his advice.

Racial tensions were running high in the community. The federal court hearing had been contentious, and we were still waiting for the judge to render his decision. Expulsions and suspensions were becoming an issue as the number of black students expelled and suspended soared. While white board members supported strong disciplinary action, Doris Lockhart frequently voted against the expulsion of black students, contributing to the perception that whites were putting blacks out of school without justification. This was not a good time to be dismissing a black teacher.

I was not surprised to see a large crowd in the boardroom. Calvin Thomas, Jerry Dickey, Ed Robinson, Billy Williams, Terry Alexander, James Williams, Larry McCutcheon, and Rev. W. P. Diggs were present.

If the principal recommending dismissal were white, we would have been in an untenable situation, but Marlene Williams is black. Marlene testified how she had received a complaint from a parent about a teacher hitting a child and dragging another across the floor. She added that all but one of the children in the room corroborated the story. Wukela could not shake her testimony. Evelyn Heyward, the previous principal at Lester, then testified how she had had a similar problem with the teacher and placed her on probation. Evelyn also held up well during the cross-examination.

The parents of the two children who had been hit and dragged across the floor testified. They were adamant about not wanting the teacher to teach their children any more. Both said their children were doing better in a room with a first-year teacher.

A licensed practical nurse from the school testified that she saw the teacher drag a student across the floor. Another school nurse and a teacher testified that the teacher had trouble controlling her class.

The dismissal hearing was similar to a trial with the lawyers representing the school administration and the teacher questioning each witness. The hearing differed from a trial in that each witness also had to respond to questions from board members. With so many people asking questions, it was 8:00 when the last witness finished.

Since Chair Anna Rose Rainwater had said she was going to stop at 8:30, no matter what, Steve Wukela asked that he be allowed to wait and begin his defense at a second meeting. The board agreed and set May 1 as the date to continue the hearing.

I had mixed feelings about breaking off the hearing. Like everyone else, I didn't relish the idea of staying late into the night. But the delay put our case at a disadvantage in two ways. First, the teacher's lawyer had heard our entire case. He now had time to prepare a defense to rebut our evidence. Second, the board would be hearing the defense a couple of weeks after the administration's case had been presented. I feared the most recent presentation would influence the board more than one they had heard earlier.

Anna Rose, a stickler for time, was about to start the May 1 hearing three minutes early and without Doris Lockhart, the only black member. "You don't want to do that," I told Anna Rose. Doris strolled in precisely at the beginning time.

The teacher was the first witness for the defense. After Wukela led her through a series of questions, we knew she had grown up in Florence because her grandmother wouldn't let her take the train back to her New Jersey home following a train accident; she had worked forty hours a week at a grocery store while in high school yet finished in the top 10 percent of her class; and she married, divorced, raised two children, and worked two jobs all while completing college.

The teacher spoke of her dedication to teaching, explaining how she worked beyond what was required of her. She then explained away the documentation in her record, saying the charges were not true, but she had not wanted to confront her principal about them.

I didn't get angry until she said that we recommended dismissal only after learning she wasn't a member of the SCEA and wouldn't have representation.

She accused us of threatening to take away her teaching certificate unless she resigned.

A series of parents and school staff followed the teacher to the stand, testifying to her dedication. While the witnesses didn't say she was an outstanding disciplinarian, the general tone was that her classes were no worse than those of the average teacher. None of the parents who testified had children in the teacher's class, and they were not speaking from firsthand experience with her.

Wukela questioned the erosion of teacher authority, asking all his witnesses if they didn't think it would be better if teachers had the right to paddle their students.

Mary Davis, a parent, drew laughter from the board and the audience when she testified that she told the principal to beat her son Thomas, saying, "If teachers be scared of these students, we ain't going to have nobody to teach them." She added, "If pinching and hitting don't kill them, put it back in. The child has to respect the teacher. If they put beating back in, I'll be the first to sign up."

Mrs. Davis went on to talk about a teacher at the school who "passed out." When Wukela asked why, she said, "Because of my son," and the audience roared.

Other defense witnesses were a local pastor, a parent who had a child in the teacher's class, the school's computer lab manager, the school custodian, and an assistant from the autistic class. None of the witnesses claimed the teacher was outstanding.

Frank Gilbert, a former state senator and the field representative for the South Carolina Education Association, testified last. After establishing his credentials as a labor specialist, Gilbert talked about other incidents in the district where teachers, according to him, had done worse things than this teacher, saying these other teachers should be fired before her. Most of these accusations, while having some basis in fact, were false.

Referring to a recent incident, Gilbert said a white teacher at South Florence High School had picked up a student and thrown him across the room. Actually the teacher had picked up a black student from behind and swung him around because the teacher thought the student was about to hit a girl.

In his most outlandish story, Gilbert claimed we caught a teacher and a student in the sex act and had done nothing about it. He may have been thinking about a teacher and student who admitted having a sexual relationship. We fired the teacher and asked that his license to teach be revoked.

I didn't recognize the "love letter" from a teacher to a student that Gilbert read. I think he made it up based on an incident involving another South Florence teacher. The teacher had written a letter to the student expressing affection but without the sexual connotation that had been added in Gilbert's version.

Gilbert closed with a story about a white male teacher who had an affair with a black girl, claiming nothing was done about it. In this case the teacher was reported to the Sheriff's Department although they never determined that he was sexually involved with the girl. The Sheriff's Department negotiated a deal with him. He was allowed to resign, and the charges against him were sealed. Principal Curt Boswell asked that his certification be revoked.

When Steve Wukela challenged the district to disprove these stories, I had a hard time staying in my seat. I wanted to contest each falsehood but realized this would only take us on a wild goose chase. Besides, we could not use any names in an open hearing.

Laurence recalled Marlene Williams to rebut some of the teacher's testimony, making it clear that it was Marlene who had asked if the teacher could be allowed to resign and that I only advised the teacher to go to the SCEA for advice. Marlene ended her testimony with a passionate statement on behalf of the children, saying she was concerned about their welfare and we needed to protect them from abuse.

Laurence's closing argument focused on the teacher's inability to manage a classroom rather than her pattern of abusing children. Wukela, as he had done throughout the hearing, talked about the need for teachers to discipline (meaning hit) children. He said suspension was worse than hitting children, seeing it as "giving up on children."

When the board adjourned at 9:15 to deliberate, I had a sinking feeling. No matter how the board decided, the situation was lose-lose for us. If the board fired the teacher, racial tensions in the district would increase; if they didn't, we would have an ineffective teacher on our hands.

The board returned to open session forty-five minutes later. Anna Rose and Doris seemed stressed, but I noticed a wry grin on Larry Orr's face. I knew we had lost.

Larry moved to suspend the teacher for the remainder of the year without pay. She was required to undergo counseling during the summer. After successfully completing counseling, she was to be reinstated as a teacher in Florence School District One, but not at Lester. The vote was 5–1 with Glenn Odom voting for dismissal.

Board members left the building quickly, Anna Rose by the back door. The teacher and her supporters hung around. When a reporter asked her for a comment, she said she wished for "everyone to be more like Jesus."

Calvin Thomas came over to me, wanting to know what we were going to do about the teacher at South Florence who "threw the black student across the room." I told Calvin we weren't going to do anything, explaining the incident was over. He warned me that I had better get the district under control or "the whole community was going up in flames."

The next day I pulled the teacher's personnel file and checked her academic record, finding that she was not in the top 10 percent of her high school class, finishing 36 out of a class of 165 and failing Algebra II twice. Neither was she an honor graduate of Francis Marion University, graduating with a 2.6 grade-point average.

I didn't make Lionel Brown, the principal of Savannah Grove, happy when I assigned him this teacher for the coming year. Threatening to resign, he complained bitterly about the difficulty of building a good program and having to take a person like this.

Before the start of the school year, we checked with the counselor whom the teacher had been seeing during the summer. The counselor surprised me by recommending that the teacher be assigned to a classroom with another teacher and continue counseling. The counselor was willing to put this recommendation in writing.

To accommodate this teacher, we would have to hire an additional teacher, a move the board was unwilling to make. At the August meeting, the board authorized me to offer the teacher a position as a classroom assistant. The teacher and her attorney accepted the offer under protest and let me know they were going to sue us for breach of contract. I reminded them that the board had required her to "satisfactorily complete counseling," which she had not done.

Two weeks after school began, Sara Slack interrupted me in a meeting to tell me that a mother and grandmother were complaining about a lady at Savannah Grove hurting a student. The teacher we had tried to dismiss, now serving as a classroom assistant, was the accused.

There was no reason for the child to concoct the story. The accusers did not know the teacher's history. Additionally, witnesses supported the child's version of the incident. It was clear that the teacher had put her hands on him.

The next day Sara Slack, Lionel Brown, and I met with the teacher and Steve Wukela. Based on his interviews of the student and the grandmother, Lionel was convinced the teacher had shaken the child. Lionel was equally upset that the teacher had complained to another teacher about how cold and unfriendly the school was. Lionel said he didn't want her back: not only had she shaken the child, but she was creating dissension at the school.

I told the teacher I was going to dismiss her. Steve Wukela asked what kind of references we would give her if she left the district. I said I would tell other superintendents the truth, but I wouldn't go out of my way to hurt her. Lionel and Sara said they would only give dates of employment.

Wukela asked, "Will you accept her resignation as a teacher?"

I agreed in order to eliminate the threatened breach of contract suit. Two days later the teacher came to my office and handed me her letter of resignation.

TWENTY-FOUR **Running the Gauntlet**

Early in March 1996, when I agreed to appear on "Tell It Like It Is," a call-in show on radio station WYNN, the community soul station, I had no idea that Clarence Alston's leaving North Vista would be an issue.

A couple of weeks earlier, Clarence had told me he was resigning. I had not asked for his resignation or even suggested he leave. Clarence had told me he had other opportunities he wanted to pursue. I understood he was tired of the controversy swirling around North Vista and suspected that he had decided the school needed a change in leadership. While I wished him well, I was glad to see him leaving.

The first sign of trouble came two days before the show. Charles Bacote, the show's host, called to say there would be a change in format. Jerry Dickey, a representative of the community, was to appear with me on the show. While I was willing to go on the show and answer questions, I was not willing to go on with a person whose purpose for being there was to attack me. I told Charles I would not participate. He said he would call his boss and get back to me. He called the next day and said I would be appearing alone.

Since I was anticipating questions on rezoning, I had asked Rick Reames to accompany me on the show. When I arrived at the station, a small cinder-block building sitting near a railroad overpass, I was surprised to find a group of about ten people carrying signs, chanting and protesting. A television truck with a big antenna was parked in front of the radio station.

Charles Bacote apologized for the "circuslike atmosphere," but he didn't do anything about it. Rick Reames, Charles, and I were in a small broadcasting booth with glass windows on two sides. While I was answering questions, a television cameraman, using high-powered lights, was shooting pictures through the glass. Someone else was taking flash pictures.

Bacote began the show with some taped comments from two of the protestors, a female preacher whose son had been expelled for bringing a knife to school, and Jerry Dickey, who wanted to know why Clarence Alston, the principal of North Vista Elementary School, was being fired. Since Alston had voluntarily resigned, I wondered why Dickey thought he was being fired.

Questions came in steadily. I answered most of them, but I was glad Rick was there to deal with those on special education. Many questions were based on false information or premises. Several Carver parents were mad about being rezoned to Delmae. Some people called about discipline issues. A couple of students called. A lady from Darlington called and couldn't understand why I couldn't answer her question about Darlington County Schools, which is a different school district.

After sixty-five minutes—the show was supposed to be an hour, but they let it run over—I was through. Before I could leave however, I had to do an interview with the television crew. When I went out the back door, the protestors created a gauntlet for me to pass through, chanting, "Tell it like it is," and "Dr. Alston is gone; you'll have to go."

I wasn't afraid. None of the protestors tried to block the path to my car. But I was angry, not so much at the protestors but at Charles Bacote and WYNN. The radio station was private property, and the station management could have kept the protestors off its property.

A couple of days later, Charles Bacote called and asked me to appear on the show again. I prided myself in being willing to take on tough issues and was not going to run and hide. However, I wasn't going to be abused as I had been on the first appearance. After making it clear I expected to be treated better, I agreed to the second show.

When I did the second show on April 14, there were no demonstrators, no television cameras, and no newspaper reporters.

One of the complaints I had heard during the first program was that I was not accessible. Taking the initiative, I announced a plan to be available in my office to take the phone calls from the public on Wednesday afternoons. I would not refer these calls to staff members but would take them personally.

The call-in questions were steady but not hostile. Topics were rezoning, discipline, respect for cultural differences, and the quality of education in the district. At the conclusion of the program, Charles Bacote thanked me for coming back and praised my willingness to personally take questions on Wednesday afternoons.

Even though I had won Bacote over, Charles Foxe and Elder James Williams were still angry. Both spoke at the April 1996 board meeting. Foxe took issue with board member Dick SoJourner over a letter published in the *Florence Morning News*. In his letter Dick had complained about the pressure from special interest groups, especially minorities. Dick also wrote that the board was forced to spend money on "frivolous legal problems." Things would really be lively if Foxe, a candidate for the school board, were elected.

James Williams asked the board to do all it could to keep Clarence Alston at North Vista Elementary School. Since I knew that Williams talked with Alston regularly, I couldn't understand why he thought Alston was being forced out.

While I appreciated the difficulty of Alston's position at North Vista, I was not about to try to change his mind about leaving. With the Justice Department ordering changes at North Vista, it was a good time for a new principal.

Later that month I went with Pam McDaniel, the district's director of public information, to North Vista to meet with parents about hiring a new principal. We met with a focus group in which the main question was, what characteristics do you want in a new principal? Since I thought these parents would respond better to Pam than to me, I asked her to lead the session—a good decision because the group was testy, challenging the procedure, wanting to know what was going to happen next, and arguing over semantics. I could not have handled the seventy-five-minute session as calmly as Pam did.

At the end of the process, the group decided that the principal needed to be an African American male. I wondered how they would have felt if a predominantly white group identified gender and race as the most important characteristics for a new principal.

Two days later I talked with Clarence Alston, wanting to put to rest the rumors that he was being forced to leave. I was surprised to learn that he had not decided on a job, sitting on two offers.

I selected Sharon Dixon, a thirty-two-year-old, black assistant principal at Moore Intermediate School, to replace Alston at North Vista and recommended her to the board at the May meeting. When we came out of the executive session, I found a note from Charles Foxe at my place, asking that the current principal at Johnson Middle School in neighboring Timmonsville, who was also a former assistant principal at Wilson High School, be appointed to the North Vista job. While I liked this man, I had not considered him a top candidate because he lacked experience in elementary schools.

When I left the meeting that night, Charles Foxe, John Carey, and Jerry Dickey were waiting for me beside my car, upset that their candidate had not been appointed. I listened to them and told them I recommended the person I thought best for the position. I assured them they would like Sharon.

School boards hire superintendents to run the school districts. Principals work under the direction of the superintendent to implement board policy and programs. I think Clarence Alston forgot for whom he worked. While it is important to involve parents, Clarence seemed to be taking his direction from some vocal community members, not from me.

When I hired Sharon Dixon to become principal of North Visa, I hoped things would improve at that school. But I wasn't going to depend on hope. I talked to Sharon about my expectations. I warned her that people in the community would try to dominate and control her. While we both understood the importance of parental support, we also agreed that the school should be for the children. I advised her to concentrate on educational issues and avoid the political alligators who try to use the schools for their purposes.

What Are You Going to Do with Carver?

TWENTY-FIVE

What are you going to do with the old Carver? That was a question frequently asked during our campaign to pass a bond referendum for the new schools. We couldn't answer that question because we had not decided. Once the funding for the new school was in place, we had to address the issue of old Carver's future.

For several years the school district had operated an alternative school for students who had been expelled from traditional schools, but the district lacked a permanent home for this school, moving it from one location to another. Old Carver looked liked a good candidate to become that permanent home.

But Carver community leaders had other aspirations for the school. On April 25, 1996, several members of my staff and I met with Teresa Ervin, Roy Cunningham, Harriet Smith, and Jimmy Harrison, representatives of the Northwest Community Council, to discuss the future of the old Carver Elementary School. My objective was to gain acceptance from the community representatives to use the old Carver School as the site for the Alternative School.

The Northwest Community people agreed to our placing the Alternative School at Carver, but they wanted additional services, such as community and adult education, job training, extended day care, and so forth. To achieve this goal, we identified various agencies that might deliver these services and invited representatives of these agencies to our next meeting.

Two weeks later representatives of the Pee Dee Regional Transportation Association, the Alternative School, the Department of Juvenile Justice, Poynor Adult Education Center, and Head Start joined the original planning group. Each agency representative expressed an interest in using the building. Mayor Frank Willis also attended and offered to put a twenty-four-hour police substation at the school, laying to rest the concern about security. We agreed to meet again in two weeks at Carver School to talk about the plans with the community.

The few people who attended the meeting at Carver heard a strong case for our project. Roy Cunningham, who three years earlier had called for my resignation, made strong, supportive comments about the concept and my efforts to establish the community center. Representatives of adult education, Head Start, the Alternative School, the police department, and the health department spoke of possible services for a community center.

The audience nodded and smiled at the presentation, but several raised questions. Charles Foxe wanted to know if we planned to make any renovations to the building. Harriet Smith, who had served on the planning committee, asked how we could have classes for young children (Head Start) in the building when we had just built a new school to get them out of it. The Head Start director, Darnelle Baptiste, came to my rescue, saying Head Start typically operates programs in abandoned schools.

City councilman Billy Williams talked about how unfair the rezoning was to the community. He also stated the Northwest Community should have control of the building. I thought we might be better off if we gave it to them.

Like an old boat, this project periodically seemed to spring leaks that threatened to sink it. Two days later Roy Cunningham, Teresa Ervin, Harriet Smith, and Jimmy Harrison sent me a letter saying they would support the Carver Community Center only if a black was hired to supervise it. They were reacting to comments I made to Trish Caulder, the director of adult education, in a meeting, asking her if she could find some money in her program to hire a director. The Northwest Community Council people thought I was directing her to hire somebody. The letter's most disturbing aspect was a reference to a tape of our meetings. Someone had been taping them.

I wasn't worried about a tape. I had said nothing in those meetings that I would not want made public, but the low level of trust that leads someone to tape surreptitiously a planning meeting for a community center disturbed me.

In early August the program got a big boost from Bruce Barragan, the CEO of McLeod Regional Medical Center. Bruce offered to put $300,000 to $500,000 into the center to provide health services. When I told him the health department was already involved, he said, "Fine. We can do a joint program."

At the September meeting Bruce volunteered to give the school district $50,000 for the operation of the center, solving the problem of how we were going to pay for a building manager. Later in the month we announced the gift at a press conference in front of the school. The Northwest Community Council was conspicuously absent.

Afterward, Pam McDaniel told me she tried to get Roy Cunningham to come to represent the community at the press conference. Roy refused, telling Pam they were "snubbing" the conference.

The *Pee Dee Times* manufactured a crisis by running an article saying the operation of the center was being put in jeopardy by the district's insistence on putting a white person in charge. The *Times* was referring to Carolyn Frate, coordinator of volunteers for the district, who had an office at Poynor Adult Education Center. When we were searching for a way to provide supervision for the building, we had talked of moving Carolyn to Carver since she was already on staff.

The *Pee Dee Times* article also accused me of insisting that McLeod's $50,000 go to the district rather than to the community—an absolutely false accusation. When Bruce Barragan offered the $50,000, I had no prior knowledge that he was going to do so. Additionally, the Northwest Community Council had no status as a tax-exempt organization, making it ineligible to receive a donation from McLeod's.

I suspected that Teresa Ervin was the person taping our meetings. She confirmed my suspicions when we met with Roy Cunningham to work out the supervision of the building. She put a tape recorder on the coffee table in my office as we began the meeting. I looked at the recorder but said nothing about it.

I began by saying, "I am committed to the project and don't want to see it scuttled. Let's see if we can resolve our concerns and move forward. I would especially like to hear from you."

Teresa said, "I'm concerned about the job description. I thought we had approved it and now you're trying to change it."

"I don't think we need a person with a college degree to manage the building, nor do I think we can afford to pay at that level," I responded.

Roy jumped in. "I agree with you. I don't think it takes a college degree to manage a building."

I pulled out the job description I had written. Although the title was "coordinator," the qualifications were those of a secretary. Both Roy and Teresa liked the job description. Roy said, "It will make a difference if we were talking about a salary of $250 a month or $1,000 a month."

Since I had been thinking of a monthly salary around $1,500, my stomach did a back flip. I said, "I was thinking of a salary of $1,000 a month or perhaps a little more." Teresa and Roy smiled and nodded approvingly. As we reviewed the job description, Roy suggested we change the title from "coordinator" to "manager," a change I liked and accepted.

Preparatory to opening the clinic at Carver, McLeod's planned a community meeting at the school in late September. I was asked to preside, and although I thought it would be better for someone from McLeod's to fill this function, I agreed.

This meeting was not boycotted. Many black community leaders attended— Mel Gibbs, Larry McCutcheon, Billy Williams, Charles Foxe, and others. Teresa Ervin, who worked at McLeod's, made the welcoming remarks, giving credit to the Northwest Community Council for starting the community center. She did admit the school district had been cooperative.

The bulk of the meeting was a public forum in which the community was given a chance to express desires and concerns about health services. The second question asked was, What's going to be the color of the director of the health center?

Rev. Larry McCutcheon made a plea for a gym to be built at the center. Harriet Smith, who had been involved in every step of the planning since the initial meeting, made an emotional speech about involving the community. Before the eighty-minute meeting was over, Billy Williams again accused the district of lying about rezoning.

In October the planning committee unanimously approved the job description for the center manager. When we discussed the role of the planning committee, Bruce Barragan spoke up and said it should be advisory with the final authority resting with the school board. Since Bruce was our main financial contributor, no one challenged his comments. At the conclusion of the meeting, I was asked to draw up bylaws for the committee.

Teresa Ervin, Harriet Smith, Trisha Caulder, and I served on the interview team to select the manager for Carver Community Center. Mrs. Smith, an elderly woman, was not accustomed to interviewing. Even though we had planned the questions we wanted to ask the candidates, she started asking personal questions like, "Are you married?" or "Do you have children?" None of the candidates showed any reluctance to answer these questions, but when we had a break, I asked Mrs. Smith not to ask these questions, fearing legal repercussions if asked of the wrong candidate.

Of the seven candidates interviewed, I found four acceptable. We couldn't afford my first choice, but Harriet and Teresa didn't like her much anyway. They favored a lady they knew. She wasn't bad, but Trish and I preferred a third candidate, also female. We agreed to interview these two a second time, after checking references.

In late October, in a Carver Community Center planning committee meeting, Teresa Ervin suggested that, if we didn't find the right person to hire as the manager of the center, we should put Glenn Jones, the coordinator of the Alternative School, in charge. With Glenn sitting in on the meeting, it was an awkward moment, but I responded that we couldn't do that because Glenn had a full-time job where we needed him. Glenn grinned sheepishly but said nothing. Since he missed an opportunity to take his name off the table, I decided he was campaigning for the job.

About a week later, on the day I was scheduled to interview the two finalists, board member Doris Lockhart called to suggest we hire Glenn Jones to serve in a joint position. I told her that Glenn had a full-time job and was not being considered for this one.

Doris continued to push, and I pushed back, saying, "Hiring a manager is an administrative decision."

She lost it. "I knew I couldn't talk with you. You are closed to anything that a black person wants. I'm a board member, and I'm offended that you bring up my getting into administrative decisions. I've never asked you to do anything for me."

I apologized for being abrupt and then said, "I involved Teresa Ervin and Roy Cunningham in developing the job description that had been agreed to. After it was approved, they started attacking it. Why did they approve it if they disagreed?"

"Since Teresa works at McLeod's she thinks her word should be given more weight, but she thinks you don't listen to her."

I countered, "Bruce Barragan is also a member of our advisory committee, and he has no problems with what we are doing."

Doris continued to push. "Why don't you challenge Glenn by hiring him a secretary and giving him both responsibilities?"

I refused.

Later in the day Glenn called, assuring me he was not involved in promoting himself for the position. I told him that, after talking with him at a board visit to the Alternative School, Billy Isgett had called me pushing him for the position as center manager. Glenn admitted he had expressed an interest in the job to Billy.

I said, "I don't know what you are saying, but people are hearing that you are interested in the job and I'm standing in the way." Glenn didn't have an answer to such a direct confrontation. He had called to smooth things over. I didn't feel any better. He probably felt worse.

I dreaded the interviews with the two finalists like a trip to the dentist, worrying that Glenn's name would come up again. It didn't.

After we finished the interviews, Harriet Smith wanted to know what we would do if there were a tie vote. I told her I had deliberately chosen an even number of persons for the interview team to promote consensus. We could only hire a manager when at least three of us agreed on the choice.

After we talked about the candidates, I agreed to support their candidate, who had done better in the second interview. Teresa wanted the salary moved from $12,480 to $15,000. I agreed. I felt we had cleared a major hurdle and had the Carver Community Center on track.

As requested, I had presented proposed bylaws at the November planning committee meeting. Even though the committee nitpicked the bylaws, I had not sensed a major problem. But the Northwest Community Council people were not talking to me. They were using a back channel. At the December board meeting, I realized we had another issue.

Doris Lockhart asked that the Carver Community Center bylaws be placed on the board agenda. Doris had done a revision of the bylaws. She didn't want the center manager heading the advisory committee, a change I could accept. She also wanted to eliminate at-large members from the advisory committee and wanted the advisory committee to screen press releases and schedule the building.

I was opposed to these proposals as being cumbersome and unmanageable. I really got my back up when she started making suggestions about whom I should appoint to the advisory board, a move designed to get Trish Caulder off the board.

Most board members seemed perplexed by Doris's proposal. Only Porter Stewart commented, expressing his concern about the advisory committee undertaking the management of the center, reviewing the press releases, and scheduling the building.

Irritated and confused, I asked, "What should I do?"

Doris said, "Take my suggestions to the advisory committee for consideration."

She then asked the chair to put the item on next month's agenda.

The Carver advisory committee approved the bylaws in January. The composition of the executive committee had been a sticking point. Acting on Bruce Barragan's suggestion, we resolved the issue by deciding not to have an executive committee.

We seemed to be snakebit in our effort to hire a center manager. The person we had agreed to hire failed the Test of Adult Basic Education (TABE)—even though she had a college degree. We readvertised the position.

This time forty people applied. After screening, we gave the TABE to ten. Five passed.

None of the first three candidates excited us. The fourth spoke with passion about a vision for Carver, but I was concerned about gaps in his resume. He listed himself as a substitute teacher, but I later learned that his name had been removed from the substitute list for making a pass at a student. His last two jobs were not listed on his resume.

I favored the fifth candidate, Rev. Willie Mashack. A home visitor for the district, Mashack also pastored a church in the Carver community. When he asked if the manager's job would interfere with his ministry, Mrs. Smith reassured him with, "We go to church on Sunday, too."

When we discussed the candidates, Mrs. Smith indicated a preference for the last two. I agreed but said Mashack would be my choice. Trish and Teresa declined to comment.

I looked at Trish, expecting her to support my recommendation for Mashack. She continued her silence. I sensed a strategic battle was going on between Teresa and Trish, one that I didn't understand. Each was waiting for the other to blink.

We decided to check references before making a decision.

The fourth candidate said he would provide us with references the next day. When we had not heard from him in four days, I pushed to hire Mashack. Teresa and Harriet wanted to wait. After a week, when we still had not heard from the other candidate, they agreed to hire Mashack.

On April 16, 1997, McLeod Medical Regional Center held a ribbon cutting for its new medical facility in what had been the fifth and sixth grade wing of Carver School. The wing had been transformed from rundown classrooms to a sparkling medical facility. Bruce Barragan gave most of the credit for the project to the Northwest Community Council. Teresa Ervin, who was on the program, gave credit to the Northwest Community Council for the project and introduced several members who were in the crowd.

My former superintendent in Burlington, Dr. Brank Proffit, used to advise me not to worry about who got credit for accomplishments, but I was irritated that the school district barely received any mention at the ceremony. For several months I had led a loose coalition of individuals, shaping them into an organized group. While the school board had supported the project, I knew they would have been willing to sell the building and wash their hands of the project if I had not recommended it. In spite of Dr. Proffit's advice, I wanted credit and was peeved I didn't get any.

TWENTY-SIX **Single-Member District Hearing**

October 1996 was the month the defense of the single-member district suit began. Laurence McIntosh brought Bobby Bowers to meet with the board. Bowers, a demographer for the state, had extensive experience representing government agencies in single-member district suits and in drawing lines for these suits.

After listening to Bowers and McIntosh describe the options, the board accepted the inevitability of change and voted to seek a remedy that would bring three African Americans to the board. The plan proposed created three predominantly (about 70 percent each) African American districts and a supersized fourth district. One person would be elected from each of the African American districts; six would be elected from the fourth. The plan's advantage was that it maintained at-large characteristics for the white districts. After hearing this plan, board member Porter Stewart asked if the three black districts could be combined into one and have three representatives elected from that district, giving it an at-large flavor. The board liked and accepted Porter's suggestion.

January 24, 1997, the day of the federal court hearing in the single-member district suit, began badly for me. Ridiculing the behavior problems on our buses, the *Florence Morning News* lampooned me with a cartoon showing me in front of a school bus driven by a man in an Arab headdress with kids fighting and falling out of the bus. The caption had me saying, "Not to worry! The school bus violence cases were isolated incidents—our buses are safe." I didn't think the cartoon was fair or funny, and I was not in a good mood to testify in a federal court hearing.

Judge William Traxler presided over the trial, which was in Columbia. Bobby Bowers and I were the only witnesses for Florence District One. Watching NAACP lawyer Brenda Reddix-Smalls grill Bowers and seeing him lose his temper, I vowed to remain calm. Thinking I would testify for about five minutes, I took the stand. I was there for an hour.

Reddix-Smalls asked questions about the failure rate of black students, the lack of black teachers, the absence of blacks in gifted programs, the abundance of blacks in the Alternative School, the location of Carver School, the Justice Department, and on and on. She crafted most of her questions to solicit a yes or no answer, but answering yes or no would have left out important, subtle shades of meaning.

I refused to give yes or no answers designed to make me say things I didn't want to say. She kept trying. I kept explaining my answers in great length, expounding on my belief that good board members represent all children, refusing to say the plan was based solely on race. She became frustrated and began interrupting me. Finally Judge Traxler said, "You two are just arguing with each other. We're going to take a break."

After the break she backed off, and I was soon through.

When I got down from the stand, I was handed an urgent message to call Donna Swartz, Laurence McIntosh's secretary. I couldn't imagine what kind of emergency would require me to call her. When I reached her, she said to call my office.

Now I was really confused. Why wasn't I asked to call my office in the first place? I asked Donna if she knew what was up. She said there was a potential bus strike and that I should ask to speak to Gerald Holley.

I called the office and asked for Gerald. He was out, and I was connected to Jane Tisdale, the secretary to the finance director. She didn't know anything about a strike so she switched me to Jane Miley, the transportation department secretary. Jane said Gerald was at the warehouse meeting with bus drivers and dealing with the media. She told me paychecks were the issue.

Two bus supervisors had done their payrolls differently. One had split the holiday period into eleven and nine days; the other, ten and ten. The drivers who were getting ten days on this paycheck felt they were being shortchanged. They had called the television stations, anonymously, and said they were not going to drive the afternoon routes. During its noon news show, WPDE-TV, Channel 15, had announced that children might not get home in the afternoon because of the strike. Anxious parents jammed our office phones with calls.

The drivers had called a press conference for 1:00 to air their grievances. Since I was calling at 1:30, I couldn't get back to Florence in time to help with the situation. I went to lunch with Laurence McIntosh and Bobby Bowers and worried about the bus strike all afternoon.

In court after lunch, the plaintiff presented its case, a series of witnesses who attacked the failure rate, the percentage of black teachers, discipline practices, and student placement and assignment practices. I sat there listening, hating it.

I didn't expect the judge to make a decision on the spot, but Judge Traxler said he might not make a decision at all since the proposed plan had not been considered by the General Assembly, telling the NAACP lawyers that he didn't give advisory opinions. He asked lawyers from both sides to give him, by the next Friday, briefs suggesting how to proceed with the case.

While any change in board representation would have to be enacted by the General Assembly, the Florence County legislative delegation—the representatives and senators serving Florence County—would be the ones to make the decision since the full assembly would support the local delegation.

When the trial was over, at 3:30, I found a phone and called Pam McDaniel, the director of public information. Pam said the strike had not materialized, explaining that only four drivers were dissatisfied. One of these four had called the television stations; however none of the four had the nerve to hold the announced press conference. Children had been delivered home on time.

TWENTY-SEVEN **Bailing Out**

On March 4, 1997, the board met to consider the proposed budget for the 1997–98 school year—a budget $1.3 million in the hole.

The prospect of a budget deep in the red—as well as growing problems with rezoning, discipline, and the board—led me to a decision to leave the Florence superintendency. I had been a superintendent for almost twenty-two years, and I just didn't want to do it any more.

Over the past two years I had battled the NAACP and the U.S. Justice Department over student assignments. Although we had settled the issue, solving a twenty-six-year-old problem, neither the black nor the white community was happy with the plan. The school district was facing a single-member district suit, and I knew this would bring more changes to the board. Already eight of the nine board members who had hired me had left the board.

When Billy Isgett and Nancy Rawl replaced Larry Orr and Miriam Baldwin, the board's character changed. Both Isgett and Rawl had become interested in district activities as a result of the dispute with the Justice Department and came with specific agendas. Although not openly hostile, I felt Isgett was anti-administration and anti-me. Ignoring policies and procedures, he sometimes went into classrooms unannounced, without notifying the principal.

Board members hire the superintendent to run the school district according to their policies. During my nine years as superintendent, the Florence School District One Board of Trustees had followed that model, but the norm for board behavior changed after Billy Isgett and Nancy Rawl joined the board. Other board members began slipping into the same behaviors, becoming more involved in running things. I had stayed too long.

I had always prided myself on being tough, able to handle anything. But with the stress of my job taking its toll on me personally and professionally, I did something I never thought I'd do. I started seeing a counselor. At the first session, my frustrations with my job poured out. The counselor listened and then said, "It's sounds like you're ready for a career change."

Until she made that statement, I had never considered quitting, but once she suggested leaving, the idea kept playing over and over in my mind. I decided I was going to leave.

Before the March 4, 1997, budget study session, I informed Chair Glenn Odom of my decision. I called the press and told them to expect an important announcement at 6:45.

After the brief budget study session, I began my comments by saying I was not resigning but asking that my contract (which ran through June 30, 1998) not be renewed. I said I would begin looking for another job and might ask to be released before the end of my term. I pointed out that, as a lame duck, I might be able to make tough decisions without worrying about the consequences. Carroll Player and Glenn Odom offered words of praise, but other board members said nothing.

The next day the *Florence Morning News* ran a huge headline: "District 1 Bombshells." My resignation and the budget deficit were the bombshells. Two weeks later the newspaper attacked me in an editorial, "School District 1 Can No Longer Wait for New Leadership." According to the *Morning News,*

> District One is out of control, and someone needs to draw in the reins. Truitt appears woefully out of touch and unable—or reluctant—to do anything.
>
> Those who have rallied behind the fallen leader, attesting to his worth to the district, should look at the big, ugly picture. Whatever good has been done is greatly overshadowed, thus rendering Truitt ineffective.

Several supporters—Principal Martin Smith of Briggs Elementary School, board members Dick SoJourner and John Floyd, and others—wrote letters challenging the editorial. The newspaper did not print them immediately. After repeated calls, they printed Martin's letter in May.

Martin hit the newspaper hard for being anti–Florence School District One, saying this bias is one of the few constants in the many changes they had made at the newspaper. He chastised the paper for printing untruths, writing, "To say that Florence School District One is mismanaged, that our superintendent is out of touch, that finances are in disarray, or that there are rampant disciplinary problems is to report an untruth."

I especially liked a point made by Dan Stoddard, a parent, who in his letter said, "Regarding your main point that the administration has not used available funds wisely, the evidence clearly points in the opposite direction. In a business, a CEO that was able to produce a product of above-average quality (i.e., student performance as reflected by test scores) with such a low per-unit cost . . . would be hailed as a genius. In Florence, however, we seem to run them out of town on a rail."

Dick SoJourner asked the paper to "get off your crucifixion and be constructive, factual, and helpful."

John Floyd continued Martin Smith's theme that the paper didn't support education, writing, "Your attack on Dr. Truitt's activities is incorrect. He spends many hours each week discussing school matters with community groups. . . . Why in your reporting do you not address the real problem of our legislative delegation failing to provide equal funds for our children?"*

While I appreciated the support of the letter writers, I was devastated by the editorial attack. I could not understand why I was being attacked personally.

Until this time my career had been a straight, upward climb. I taught only three years before I was recruited to become an assistant principal. When I was twenty-six years old, I became principal of an 1,100-pupil junior high school. After three years in that job and two years in graduate school, I became an assistant superintendent in Danville, Virginia. Three years later, at age thirty-five, I was named superintendent in that district.

During the twelve years I worked in Danville, I frequently got calls from larger districts asking me to apply to become their superintendent. I stayed in Danville because of my commitment to that district and to give my son a chance to go through the K–12 system without being forced to move. I was once highlighted in the National School Board Association's newsletter as an up-and-coming superintendent.

This was the reputation I brought to Florence. Now the local newspaper was advocating that I be thrown out, even after I had indicated I would be leaving at the end of my contract.

My confidence was shattered, and I had no aspirations for the future except to get out of Florence School District One.

---

* Smith's letter was published in the *Florence Morning News* on May 6, 1997; Stoddard's on May 1, 1997; SoJourner's on May 10, 1997; and Floyd's on May 11, 1997.

Changing
TWENTY-EIGHT **Board Elections**

Each year on the first Tuesday in May, Florence School District One held a school board election. Anyone who lived in the district, was at least eighteen years old, and was a registered voter could run for the school board and vote in the school board election. Board members were elected to three-year terms.

Some years there would be as many as ten candidates in the field; on other occasions, only four or five. It didn't matter how many people ran, the top three vote getters earned a term on the school board. There was no requirement to receive a majority of the votes cast.

When I was hired by the Florence School Board, there were two African Americans on the board. Later, with the defeat of Calvin Thomas, the number was reduced to one. Since the school district was approximately half white and half black, the lack of representation on the school board irritated the black community. The local NAACP filed suit to force a change in the method of board representation from at-large to single-member district.

In a single-member district plan, the district would be divided into nine voting districts with one board member elected from each district. Under this plan, people would be able to vote for only one board seat and that person would have to reside in that district. Since Florence residential communities tended to be segregated, it would be possible to draw at least three districts in which blacks would be a majority.

On March 11, 1997, one week after I announced I was not seeking a contract extension, the board met with attorney Laurence McIntosh to discuss the single-member district suit. Laurence told the board that the Florence County legislative delegation favored a three-district plan with each district having three members.

The three-district plan was a hybrid, something between at-large and single-member district. Under this plan, the school district would be divided into three sections. Each section would be able to select three members. Given the Florence housing pattern, it would be possible to insure that one of these districts was majority black. Like the single-member plan, this plan would likely elect three black members to the board, assuming people voted based on race—which everyone was assuming. This hybrid plan became known as the 3-3-3 plan.

Initially the black district would elect two members, leaving one white district without the opportunity to vote the first year and placing incumbent board members in races against each other in a district. When Glenn Odom volunteered to give up his seat so the plan could move on, the inflammatory rhetoric started.

Dick SoJourner claimed "reverse discrimination." Billy Isgett and John Floyd joined Dick in opposing the plan.

In late April, John Floyd called me and proposed holding an executive session before the next board meeting and inviting Laurence McIntosh and Helen McFadden, a civil rights attorney from Kingstree, to meet with us. John was unhappy with Laurence McIntosh's work as our lawyer.

John must have been watching too many television shows where lawyers work miracles. He seemed to feel that if we had a different lawyer, we could win an impossible case.

I told John I didn't like the idea of a potentially long executive session before the board meeting, nor was I thrilled with bringing in another attorney to meet with our attorney. I agreed to call Chair Odom and talk with him about the situation. Odom agreed to hold a special meeting with just Laurence present.

When we met, Laurence told the board the three-district plan was dead. Judge Traxler was going to order a single-member district plan. Laurence also said Traxler was going to refer the case to Judge Margaret Seymore, a black judge stationed in Florence.

A couple of weeks later, the board met with Laurence and Bobby Bowers. I thought we would discuss lines for single-member districts, but five members— Billy Isgett, Dick SoJourner, John Floyd, Carroll Player, and Nancy Rawl— favored presenting the old 3-3-3 plan, three districts with three members each, to the court.

The board haggled. Nancy Rawl asked if Laurence could ask the court if Judge Seymore was a member of the NAACP and, if she were, suggest that the judge disqualify herself. Carroll Player later made reference to Nancy's "dumb, damn question," the only time I ever heard Carroll use profanity.

Even though she was based in Florence, I didn't know Margaret Seymore. I agreed with Carroll; it would be a bad tactical mistake to raise questions about the judge's integrity.

Billy Isgett made it clear he was primarily concerned about his seat. He asked Laurence, "Do you have a plan that puts me in a district without having to run against an incumbent? If you don't, I plan to introduce such a plan myself."

Shifting gears, Billy continued. "I have contacted Helen McFadden, who said she would appeal the single-member district suit for $10,000. I think we need to fight this thing."

When I had come to Florence, I had worked with the board to clarify roles and responsibilities. Every board member knew they had no authority as individuals, but Billy, on his own, was contacting an attorney on behalf of the board.

Dick SoJourner changed the outcome of the meeting when he said, "I came to this meeting in favor of single-member districts, but I now want the 3-3-3 plan." With Dick's switch, the majority of the board favored a plan that had no chance.

Before the board voted, I spoke up for Doris Lockhart, who was absent. "Doris regrets very much that she couldn't be here tonight, and she asked me to tell you how concerned she is about the 3-3-3 plan. She opposes it. She told me that she feels we'll lose the good will and support of the black community and delegation if we continue to pursue the 3-3-3 plan." Anna Rose and Porter chimed in, supporting everything I had said. Still, the "Fighting Five" would not back off.

The next day I called Laurence to find out what he was going to do. He said Brenda Reddix-Smalls went into orbit when she heard of the board's support for the 3-3-3 plan, complaining that she would now have to prepare a different case since the board was fighting the single-member plan. She emphasized to Laurence that this would cost time and money.

Discouraged, Laurence admitted to me that he was bothered by the specter of another lawyer out there talking with the board members about appealing the case. He called the next day and said he had talked with Glenn about being relieved from the case, saying he was unable to defend the board's position.

Two things happened to change Laurence's mind. First, the hearing was changed to a status conference, which gave him more time to prepare a defense since there would be no testimony. Second, Dick SoJourner reversed his position and decided to support single-member districts.

Why Dick changed his mind is anybody's guess. A lone wolf on the board, Dick was volatile, subject to changing his mind for little or no reason that I could discern.

Early in June, Billy Isgett called wanting to know the status of the case. I told him Laurence thought the matter was working toward a resolution with the experts ironing out the difference in the two, single-member district plans. He asked, "How do you feel about it?"

I said, "It's useless to fight when you are going to lose anyway, and you will destroy good will in the process." Billy said he agreed with me. I hung up thinking Billy would support the single-member district plan.

Two days later the board met to discuss the single-member district suit. Laurence and Glenn wanted the meeting held in open session, but Carroll Player made a motion to go into executive session. The motion failed with John and Nancy voting with Carroll.

Laurence reported that Brenda Reddix-Smalls and he had met with Judge Seymore the previous week. Noting the single-member district plans submitted by the NAACP and the board were similar, Seymore asked the map experts, Bowers and Roulff (the plaintiff's map expert), to meet and resolve the differences. Laurence brought the plaintiff's plan to the meeting. If approved by the board, the case would be settled.

Before showing the plan, Laurence reviewed the history of school board elections in Florence. In the 1960s and 70s, Florence had all-white boards. Theodore Lester, the first black member, was appointed to the board when Dr. Julian Price resigned. In June 1978 the NAACP filed suit against the method of electing board members, which at that time occurred at a town meeting. The method was changed to single-shot voting, but blacks still had a hard time being elected because of the requirement to attain a majority of the votes cast; many lost in run-off elections.

Laurence described how in 1986 board elections were changed to the at-large method in which the top three vote-getters were elected. According to Laurence, this method of electing board members is not illegal per se but can become so when certain conditions exist. If blacks represent a significant portion of the population, are geographically compact, and are politically active (that is, vote) and if whites are voting in a block, the at-large elections become suspect if black candidates are not elected.

Bringing the history up-to-date, Laurence pointed out that in 1993, three years earlier, Florence had elected three white members to the board. The following year Doris Lockhart was reelected as the only black. In the past year an all-white slate had been elected. According to a nationally recognized consultant whom Laurence had hired, whites in Florence were voting in blocks. Given this analysis, Laurence had become convinced we couldn't maintain our present system, and he had asked Bobby Bowers to become involved.

Bowers developed a plan that divided the school district into two districts for the purpose of electing board members. One district, which was twice as large as the other and majority white, would be entitled to six representatives. The other district, which was predominantly black, would be entitled to three representatives. The plan was later modified by splitting the larger district in half, leaving three districts of approximately the same size with each entitled to three representatives. The plan was called the "3-3-3 plan."

Laurence had presented this plan to Judge Traxler on January 24, 1997. Traxler refused to rule on the plan and sent it to the General Assembly. The Florence County delegation in the General Assembly could not agree on a plan. When Traxler realized the General Assembly was unable to agree on a plan, he decided to order a single-member district plan. Both the NAACP and Bowers submitted plans to Traxler.

Because of scheduling problems, Traxler assigned the case to Judge Margaret Seymore of Florence. When Dick SoJourner changed his position to support single-member districts, the majority of the board supported this approach. According to Laurence, the NAACP plan had been "cleaned up" and to continue to argue would be like arguing "Tweedledum and Tweedledee."

After Laurence finished with this background, Billy Isgett moved to go into executive session. Billy, who had voted against going into executive session in his first board meeting because he didn't like executive sessions, now wanted to talk privately. His motion failed 2–5–1, with Carroll Player supporting and John Floyd abstaining.

With the plan on the table, Glenn asked for questions.

Carroll spoke first. "I like the 3-3-3 plan. You get broader participation and better candidates. Everybody would be able to vote on a school board candidate every year, and candidates would represent larger areas. I strongly prefer this plan over single-member districts."

Nancy asked, "When are board members going to get their say in court on the advantages of the 3-3-3 plan? I thought we would have a chance to appeal to the court."

Doris asked, "How much is it going to cost us if we continue this case?"

Laurence said, "The costs are not inconsequential."

In explaining why he had changed his vote, Dick said, "I don't like any of the plans but I think we are going to lose, and I don't want to spend any more money."

Doris made the motion to settle; Dick seconded.

Not one to give up easily, Carroll Player again spoke in favor of the 3-3-3 plan, arguing that it gave voters more influence because they could participate in electing more board members. He also said the system produced stronger candidates because geographic representation was not as limited.

John Floyd spoke after Carroll. "I will abstain on this motion. I agree with Carroll that the 3-3-3 plan is better, but the NAACP has structured this case so we can't win. Common sense and reason are not being used. It's time to move forward and get this behind us."

With Anna Rose Rainwater absent, John's abstention was critical. The motion passed 4–3–1.

On July 15, 1997, the board met to vote on the consent order that Laurence had drafted based on the concept approved earlier by the board. The meeting was set for 5:00, and we were expecting eight members to attend. At 5:15 only five members were present when Billy Isgett burst into the meeting, indicating he had been told 5:15 for the meeting, angrily asking if other board members had been misinformed of the meeting time.

The board approved the consent order, but Dick, who had been the swing vote in approving the concept, and Billy voted against the resolution.

As we were leaving the meeting, John Floyd drove up, obviously confused about the meeting time.

The next day the *Morning News* article highlighted Billy's claim that he was misinformed of the meeting time. The article concluded noting, "The *Morning News* did not receive written notification of the meeting."

I asked Joanne Revell, the pubic information secretary, about the notification. She had faxed the newspaper an announcement and followed up the fax with a phone call. When the reporter told her they had not received the fax, she sent another one, which our records indicated they had received. The problem was the reporter who covered the meeting was not the one who talked with Joanne on the phone.

TWENTY-NINE A New Regime

On June 26, 1997, a year before the expiration of my contract, the board met for the first time to discuss the search for my replacement. Sissy Henry and Ellen Henderson, search consultants with the South Carolina School Boards Association, met with the board. I didn't want to attend the meeting, but Chair Glenn Odom insisted I be there.

At the beginning of the meeting, Glenn tried to resolve the issue of which board—the current one or the one to be elected in November—would hire the new superintendent. In previous discussions the board had agreed that the to-be-elected board would hire the superintendent. When Porter Stewart made the motion to formalize this agreement, it failed by a 4–4 vote, with John Floyd, Billy Isgett, Dick SoJourner, and Nancy Rawl voting against it. Anna Rose Rainwater, tired of all the board's problems, had decided not to run for reelection. She had begun missing a lot of meetings and was absent from this one.

Nancy Rawl, explaining her reasons for voting against the motion, said, "If someone with just the right qualifications were to come along, this board should be in a position to hire them." Nancy's comment revealed her unfamiliarity with the superintendent selection process, which involved advertising, screening, and interviewing. A board didn't hire someone who walked in the door, no matter how appealing the candidate.

Unable to resolve the issue of which board would do the hiring, the board moved into a discussion of focus groups. Ellen Henderson recommended the board use seven focus groups, including a white community leaders group and a black community leaders group. I thought the single-race groups were a bad idea, but Doris Lockhart, the only black on the board, supported them, and the board accepted Ellen's recommendation.

Next, Sissy Henry described a timeline for hiring the new superintendent. Although this schedule made it clear that the new board members would be hiring the superintendent, none of the board members who had voted against this raised an objection.

I was thankful the newspaper didn't cover the meeting, but the issue of the single-race focus groups did surface a couple of months later. One Friday in September, the *Morning News* ran an article about the focus groups for the superintendent's selection, highlighting the single-race groups. The article was confusing, giving little information, but quoting Glenn Odom, Doris Lockhart, and Calvin Thomas, making it appear they were arguing with each other.

Glenn was quoted as saying a 5–4 or a 6–3 board might have trouble selecting a superintendent because of race. Doris and Calvin seemed offended that anyone would suggest that race would be an issue.

In November 1997 all nine board seats were up for grabs in the newly drawn, single-member districts.

The court settlement called for a random drawing to select the terms for new board members with three districts getting one-year terms, three districts getting two-year terms, and three districts getting three-year terms. Two predominantly white districts were grouped with one predominantly black district for the drawing. The random drawing was held at the September board meeting. Laurence McIntosh asked a parent who was sitting in the front row to draw the lots.

The next day Laurence called to report a complaint from Calvin Thomas about not being informed of the drawing. Laurence had written Calvin a letter about the drawing, but Calvin claimed he hadn't received it. My secretary had called him on the day before the meeting to tell him about the drawing, and he said he would attend. Playing politics, he had called the newspaper and complained.

When the news reporter called me, I told him Calvin had been informed of the meeting. When the reporter wrote the article, he omitted this information, and Calvin's assertion that he was not informed of the drawing went unchallenged. Calvin was quoted as saying the court agreement required us to notify the NAACP of the drawing of lots, a statement with no basis in fact. We had notified Calvin as a matter of courtesy.

On September 30, 1997, the *Florence Morning News* printed a letter from a man who attacked the board and me for not involving the NAACP in the drawing of lots for the board terms. His main, but erroneous, premise was that the board was obligated by the court order to hold a drawing in a joint meeting with the NAACP.

After stating unequivocally that the court order required a joint meeting, he went on to say the "community was informed at the state NAACP meeting in Columbia that lame duck Superintendent Thomas Truitt sent a memo to

Laurence McIntosh and the school board members stating he felt it was not necessary to notify the NAACP."

I had sent no such memo. In my weekly memo to the board, I had explained that there was some confusion regarding the drawing of lots. I went on to make it clear that the court agreement did not require the NAACP to be involved. The only requirement was that the drawing be done in an open meeting.

The letter to the newspaper suggested the board had tried to sneak the drawing of lots by the NAACP and the public. Nothing could have been further from the truth.

In a letter to Eleazor Carter, NAACP attorney, Laurence informed him that the lots would be drawn in a public meeting. In a second letter, Laurence indicated the meeting would likely be on September 11—which it was. Laurence also sent a letter to Calvin advising him of the meeting, the letter that Calvin claimed he never got.

Both Rick Reames and Jerry Wilkes had talked with Calvin by phone on the day before the meeting and had told him when the drawing was being held. In addition the drawing of lots was on the board agenda, which was sent to the local media on the Friday before the Thursday meeting.

The funniest thing in the man's letter was his assertion that the NAACP was paying its attorneys' fees, while the school board was burdening the taxpayers with theirs, a hilarious claim since we got the bill for the NAACP attorneys' fees the day before the letter appeared in the paper. The bill was over $102,000.

Most people do not understand how attorneys' fees are handled in cases involving civil rights. If the plaintiff—in this case the NAACP—prevails, then the defendant—the school board—is liable for the plaintiff's attorneys' fees. If the defendant wins, the defendant is still liable for his or her own legal fees but does not have to pay the plaintiff's fees. It's a lose-lose situation for the defendants.

A couple of days later I saw Rev. Terry Alexander, a member of county council and a leader in the black community. Seeking to begin the process of bringing the black and white communities together and believing that Terry was the kind of leader who could bridge the two communities, I said, "Terry, you've won the single-member district suit, but you don't know how to accept victory. This useless fighting will make it hard for a new board to work together."

The next day Terry said he had told Calvin it was time to stop fighting. He didn't say what kind of reaction he got.

I called Calvin and left word for him to call. He didn't call. After waiting two days, I got Calvin's beeper number. A few minutes after I rang it, he returned my call, and we set an appointment.

When we met in my office, I said, "Calvin, we need to start pulling together and stop the fighting. You've won the single-member district issue. What's to be gained by this bickering?"

He responded, "I agree we don't need to keep fighting, but there's still a lot of confusion regarding changes in voting precincts. My people can't get any information."

"Maps are available at Mail Boxes Etc. for $2.50," I told him. "The election commission is preparing rosters of the voters to be available before the election. People can go to the election commission and find out what precinct they're in.

"You know that there's no mention of the NAACP in the drawing of lots for school board terms."

He agreed and said, "That's why I dropped it after I realized it wasn't a part of the order." He didn't say why he didn't bother to correct his statements to the press. I saw no reason to embarrass him by pushing the issue.

Before he left, I asked him to contact me in the future when he had a problem rather than making it a public issue. He said he would, but we didn't talk again until years after I had left Florence School District One.

The election of the new board was held on November 4, 1997. Six spots were contested. Incumbents Billy Isgett and Dick SoJourner were running unopposed, as was Dr. Joe Moyer, who had lost an earlier bid for the board.

In one district, board members Porter Stewart and Nancy Rawl opposed each other. In another district, Brynda Dillon, a white, challenged incumbent Doris Lockhart, the board's only black member. The board would be getting a minimum of four new members and could get five if Dillon defeated Lockhart. Of the new board members, at least three would be black.

As the election approached, the board struggled to function. With the possibility of wholesale changes on the board in November, introducing policy issues at the October meeting was out of the question. Policy adoption required two readings, meaning a policy was introduced at one meeting and voted on at a second meeting. I refused to introduce any policies at the October meeting, knowing that there would be a minimum of four new members sitting on the board in November. The board meeting in October was one of the shortest in history. Everyone was looking toward November and the election.

On election night I went to bed with no idea of the results. When I picked up the paper in the morning, a huge headline screamed, "New Board: 5 White, 4 Black."

All incumbents, including Doris Lockhart, who had run in a majority white district, had been reelected. The new members were James Littles, a retired assistant principal; Freddie Williams, executive director of the community action council; Pat Evans, a social worker; and Dr. Joe Moyer, an allergist. All but Moyer are black.

Since I was leaving at the end of the school year, I was not concerned about the personalities that would be serving on the board. I didn't know any of the new members but was pleased that the board would now be more representative of the community's racial composition. I also thought it interesting that all incumbents were reelected with the exception of Nancy Rawl, who was defeated by another incumbent. I wondered why, if the former board had been doing such a bad job, all incumbents were reelected.

Single-member district proponents had argued that this method of electing board members would increase voter turnout. It didn't in this election, where the heaviest voting was in District 7, which had two incumbents and a challenger running. Porter Stewart defeated Nancy Rawl, 555 to 447. Although she lost, Nancy Rawl's 447 was the second only to Porter in the overall voting. The same number of votes in any other district would have elected her.

Freddie Williams in District 3 was elected with the fewest votes, 218. Fewer than 600 votes were cast in this district.

Doris Lockhart's victory over Brynda Dillon was surprising, since the district is two-thirds white. Not only did Doris win, her margin of victory was over 100 votes, 397 to 294.

Pat Evans received 226 votes to defeat two other black women whose combined votes did not equal hers. James Littles received 335 votes to defeat two other black men in District 4, where over 700 votes were cast.

Board chair Glenn Odom recorded the most one-sided win, defeating his opponent by 323 votes.

The low number of votes in this election was surprising. In theory, single-member districts bring politics closer to the grassroots level and result in greater voter participation. Ironically, no one in this election received more than 555 votes, and a couple of members were elected with fewer than 250 votes. In 1977 Freddie Jolley had received 5,700 votes, which had not been enough to elect him.

Having been hired by an at-large board, I had mixed feelings about the change from at-large to single-member districts. Without question, I would have preferred keeping the at-large system. Like some board members, I believed the at-large system was superior to single member because it kept every voter in the school district involved every year. Additionally, I defined a "good" school board member as one who is concerned about all children. I worried that members elected from single-member districts would focus narrowly on the needs of their district. I also recognized that the establishment of single-member districts meant I would have to leave the district, believing a new board would want to and should hire a new superintendent.

With a significant African American population, I thought the at-large system should be workable in Florence, but frustrated by their historical failure to get elected, blacks had not been turning out in large numbers for school board elections.

Although I considered myself fair, I realized that I was not going to be able to overcome the sense of exclusion felt by the African American community over their lack of representation on the board. Since the at-large system was not working, it had to be changed.

Two days after the election, I held an orientation meeting for the board. I did most of the talking, explaining operating procedures, trying to give board members some idea of what to expect. I also emphasized the importance of ethical behavior, pointing out that only they could police themselves.

With so many new members coming on the board at one time, I anticipated problems in getting them to function as a team. I talked about the importance of confidentiality of executive sessions. I pleaded for them to support principals in discipline cases. I advised them to stay out of administrative matters, particularly those involving student discipline at the school level.

Earlier in the day the *Morning News* editorial had proclaimed, "Florence Dist. 1 Can Get On with Its Real Business—School." The editorial went on to defend its "5–4" headline, saying headlines "are designed to tell readers at a glance what the gist of the story is."

The editorial quoted new member Pat Evans as saying, "Parents are tired of race issues separating us. It is our responsibility as adults to be fair," to which the editorial writers said, "Amen." In her first year as a board member, Pat would demonstrate an unusual perspective on fairness, beginning with her first disciplinary hearing.

Before its first regular meeting, the board held two expulsion hearings. The first involved a fifteen-year-old male who had gotten in a fight in auto-mechanics shop. In the process he had thrown a seven-pound wrench at the other student, hitting him in the back.

Freddie Williams wanted to know where the teacher was. Pat Evans asked the boy, "What would you have done differently if you had been the teacher?"

These two questions bothered me. These new board members were looking to make the teacher the scapegoat for this kid throwing a wrench at another student. The teacher was in the room when it happened, but even if he had not been, that would not have excused the student's behavior.

Freddie Williams asked, "Do you think you've done anything wrong?" The boy said, "No."

After a twenty-minute hearing, the board voted 7–2 to expel. Evans and Williams voted in the minority.

The second case also involved a fifteen-year-old male who had been recommended for a second hearing the previous spring. Fearing expulsion, the mother had never scheduled the hearing. Although the student had failed the eighth grade, the mother had temporarily beaten the system by enrolling the boy at South Florence High School, where he was failing every course.

When SFHS officials discovered the boy was not supposed to be there, they told the student he would have to attend the Alternative School. His mother thought this was unfair. At one point in the hearing, she started to walk out, only to be calmed by Pat Evans, who assured her that *she* would listen to her.

Pat may have listened, but like the other board members, she voted for expulsion. Freddie Williams raised the only issue, wanting to know why we couldn't provide transportation to the Alternative School.

One week later, when the board held its first regular meeting, Porter Stewart was elected chair; Doris Lockhart, vice-chair; and Billy Isgett, secretary. Glenn Odom wanted to serve a second term as chair, but he could not muster the votes.

Former board members John Floyd, Carroll Player, and Nancy Rawl were recognized at the beginning of the meeting. John and Carroll were both emotional, fighting back the tears. Carroll praised the district office staff. John told the board, "You will receive unfair criticism, especially from people who have never been involved before."

THIRTY Attorneys' Fees

The special school board election in November 1997 settled the board representation issue, but the question of the plaintiff's attorneys' fees was unresolved. The
NAACP attorneys had asked for $102,000 in fees. Laurence McIntosh, as board
attorney, had appealed the request to Judge Traxler, who had reduced the fees to
$64,000.

Just before the winter break in December 1997, Eleazor Carter, the NAACP
attorney, called Laurence McIntosh to discuss the fee issue. He said, "We don't
want to see this fee issue dragged out through the courts. If you could up your
offer a bit, we would be willing to forego our appeal of the judge's ruling."

Laurence responded, "We have a judge's order, and that's what we intend to
pay."

At the December meeting, the board met in executive session, giving new
board members the chance to discuss the attorneys' fees in the case that had
resulted in their election.

Jim Littles was the first to suggest paying the full amount of the request.
"What is the possibility that the plaintiff will appeal? If they do, don't we run the
risk of spending more in defending ourselves than if we paid the full amount
now?"

Freddie Williams didn't beat around the bush. He said, "I think the district
should pay the full amount because it was wrong to fight the single-member district suit. Your position was morally wrong, and now you should pay."

Doris Lockhart asked, "Who decided to appeal the fee charge?"

Glenn Odom and Dick SoJourner remembered a meeting in which the board
directed Laurence to appeal. They were wrong. When we received the bill for
attorneys' fees, I had called Glenn, who told me he was going to talk with other
board members about the appeal. Later he called me back and told me to go
ahead with the appeal. I assumed all board members wanted to appeal. Now with
Doris questioning the decision, I doubted Glenn had talked with Doris.

I sat silently, choosing not to correct Dick and Glenn's version of the appeal. I saw no reason to get into that issue. Our attorney, by his action, had made it possible for the board to save $38,000. I couldn't understand why anyone would question the decision to appeal.

Freddie Williams, directing his question to Laurence, asked, "What will you charge to handle this appeal?"

Laurence said, "It would not be inconsequential."

In the awkward silence that followed, I looked to returning board members Porter Stewart, Dick SoJourner, and Billy Isgett to speak up, but they said nothing.

Finally a new member, Dr. Joe Moyer, said, "Look. We have a judgment that saves us $38,000. While I agree with Doris that the decision to appeal should be a board decision, I think we need to go on, pay the bill, and move on. After all, it will cost the plaintiff to appeal, and I don't think they will. Let's put this thing behind us and move on."

No one challenged Moyer, and the board returned to open session. The next day I asked our business department to write the check for $64,000.

On January 20, 1998, the board held a special meeting at the request of Laurence McIntosh. Preparing for a conference call on January 22 with Judge Traxler and the NAACP lawyers, Laurence wanted direction from the board whether to maintain the position of paying only the $64,000 or to negotiate a settlement of fees.

Laurence said he did not have strong evidence for the reduced fees. At the same time he did not recommend settling for the full amount or negotiating for a lesser amount. Laurence was experiencing the ambiguity that superintendents with split boards know too well. It's easy to work for a single boss, but when you work for a board of nine people and they don't agree on basic issues, it's hard to give sound advice. Fence straddling becomes the behavior of choice.

Once again board member positions divided along racial lines—the black members wanting to pay the full amount or negotiate a settlement, the white members not willing to pay any more than required by the judge.

The position of the new board members flabbergasted me. While I expected some differences on personnel and student discipline issues, I had not anticipated that new board members would advocate paying NAACP lawyers more than we were required. Clearly the new board members saw themselves as representing the interests of the black community, not the community as a whole.

Even though the positions were clear from the beginning of the meeting, the discussion dragged on and on. James Littles argued we were wasting money by fighting the full payment, while Freddie Williams said we were obligated to pay the NAACP lawyers because the board had taken the morally wrong position.

Pat Evans saw her position as being for the children, saying, "When are we going to think of the children?"

Finally James Littles made a motion to pay the full amount requested by the lawyers. Freddie Williams seconded. The motion was defeated 4–5. No whites voted for the motion. No blacks voted against it.

A week later the *Morning News* carried a front-page story, "Judge Will Decide Fee for NAACP Lawyers." Although the meeting had been open, the newspaper had not been present when the board discussed attorneys' fees. I wondered how they got the information for the article.

Dick SoJourner was quoted as saying, "I thought the judge ruled fairly. . . . If the NAACP is so concerned about Florence School District One providing a good education, why don't they accept what the judge said?"

Calvin Thomas was quoted as saying the board was going to cost the taxpayers money by continuing to fight the fees, saying the issue was taking a toll on the district's chances of gaining community support on some crucial issues.

James Littles, showing his identification with the NAACP, said, "If I give you a bill for $100,000, why should I take anything less? We have enough problems trying to choose a new superintendent. In the meantime the interest is going clickity-clickity-clickity."

Laurence McIntosh countered Littles's reference to interest by saying, "It's not a liquidated final sum until the judge issues his order. But if the NAACP's attorneys choose to hassle about it, it could be a problem. They should take what the judge says and be done with it."

The newspaper article also raised the issue of conflict of interest for three members of the board who were members of the NAACP. According to Gary Baker, director of the ethics commission, there is no conflict of interest unless the members are voting on something that directly affects the economic interests of the NAACP. He did not see money being paid to the lawyers as a direct interest.

On the same day of the newspaper article, Judge Traxler issued a revised order, restoring $4,125 to the NAACP attorneys. Laurence called to ask me to cut a check for the new amount.

The next day I found out who leaked the information to the press. Talking with Dick SoJourner in my office, I wondered out loud who contacted the newspaper. Dick said he gave the information to them.

A strong fiscal conservative, Dick had gotten mad at the new board members because they were talking among themselves about a raise in board pay. The next day he had called Wade Jeffords at the newspaper and told him about the meeting.

During the first week in February, Laurence called to say the NAACP had appealed. Eleazor Carter had suggested the board pay the amount ordered by the judge and let the NAACP appeal any amount above that. Laurence refused. Laurence also told Carter that the board owed no interest on any fees now because an order is not a judgment, and interest is only paid on a judgment.

The board paid no additional fees.

Superintendent Search

The new board members wasted no time in beginning the superintendent search. Less than two weeks after taking office, the board met with Ellen Henderson of the South Carolina School Boards Association (SCSBA) to hear a report on the results of the focus group discussions. According to Ellen, the district had a negative image. The groups wanted a superintendent with high moral character, vision, and successful experience in other school districts.

One week later the featured editorial in the *Morning News* was "Superintendent Needs to Work on District's Image." A tacky cartoon, showing a prospective superintendent having his eyes checked for vision, accompanied the editorial.

For the first time in over ten years, due to another commitment, I missed a board meeting, one in which the board met with Sissy Henry of SCSBA to discuss procedures for hiring a superintendent. The next day, when I heard a report on the meeting, I was glad I had been absent.

Pam McDaniel, director of public information, was distressed by James Littles, who ordered her to retrieve something for him from her office. According to Pam, Littles said, "We're going to run things now."

At the conclusion of the meeting, Littles fussed about having meetings on Monday nights, the night of his standing pinochle game. He proposed limiting board meetings to Tuesdays and Thursdays, making a point of saying administrators would have to meet the board's schedule.

In mid-January 1998, the board met with Sissy Henry to screen superintendent candidates. From a pool of thirty-three, they selected ten for interviews. Three of the ten withdrew. Of the seven remaining candidates, only one was a superintendent in South Carolina, and he was from a district with fewer than one thousand students. Two were superintendents in North Carolina; one, a South Carolina assistant superintendent; one, an area superintendent from Charleston; one, the superintendent of the Department of Defense Schools in Columbia; and Allie Brooks, principal of Wilson High School.

Paul Shaw, superintendent of York School District One and a friend, had withdrawn. He called to tell me that he had applied for the wrong reasons and was now convinced he should stay in York. During our conversation he told me that Billy Isgett had called him the day after the finalists were selected to tell him he was among the finalists. Paul asked me for Billy's number so he could tell him he was withdrawing.

On Monday, February 23, 1998, the Florence School District One Board met to narrow the superintendent candidates for a second interview. Using a weighted ranking system, the board ranked the top three as follows: David Bryant, superintendent of Edgecombe County, North Carolina; Joseph Nelson, superintendent of Bertie County, North Carolina; and Allie Brooks, principal of Wilson High School.

The board had planned to select three candidates for a second interview, but when Allie Brooks ranked third, Freddie Williams and Pat Evans objected. They didn't want to interview Allie. James Littles and Doris Lockhart, the other two African American board members, supported Williams and Evans. Dick SoJourner, who at the beginning of the process had told me he would never vote for Allie, took exception. Dick argued that Allie should be given a second interview. Freddie Williams said he wouldn't come if Allie got a second interview.

The discussion became heated, and Dick got mad and walked out.

The next day Glenn Odom declared it the worst meeting he had ever been in—which was saying a lot because we had been in some bad ones together.

I was surprised by the attitude of the black members of the board. I had assumed Allie, a black man, would have their support and his only obstacle to becoming superintendent would be white member support. Obviously, Allie had some support from white members or he would not have come out third in the rankings. I had no idea why Freddie Williams was opposed to Allie.

The next night we had a disciplinary hearing and a budget study session. The board decided to resolve the unsettled issue of which candidates to interview. Freddie Williams stayed for the disciplinary hearing. At the beginning of the budget session, Williams got up and left without saying a word to anyone. He returned near the end of the session in time to participate in the board discussion of superintendent candidates.

I did not stay for the discussion of the candidates, but the headlines the next day read, "2 Vie for Dist. 1 Schools Chief." The vote had been 8–1 to eliminate Allie from consideration. Dick SoJourner had been the lone board member to vote for Allie's inclusion in the round of second interviews.

Board chair Porter Stewart was upset with the article because reporter Wade Jeffords had told him that the announcement would not be in the morning paper. Porter had wanted the opportunity to tell Allie before he read it in the paper.

The following day's headlines startled the community. "Candidates Unfairly Dropped" splashed across the top of the front page in bold, one-inch-high letters. Dick SoJourner had gone to the newspaper with the story of the black school board members opposing Allie.

Dick argued the board was obligated to select three finalists. He was wrong. The purpose of the weighted voting was to give a sense of direction to the board. They could have selected two, three, four, or even more candidates, if they chose.

Three days later the Sunday editorial, "Trustees Refute SoJourner's Account," quoted Pat Evans as saying SoJourner's statement was a "point-blank lie." Doris Lockhart was quoted as saying, "I supported Mr. Brooks. This has caused much anguish. What (SoJourner) did was try to divide and conquer."

The editorial went back to Evans. "Until action is taken against SoJourner, I can't see going any further with more interviews." Littles agreed, "I think we ought to quit everything until we iron out that problem."

Black members were saying they had supported Allie Brooks and were calling SoJourner a liar. They feared they would lose the support of their constituency if the truth were known since Allie was popular in the black community. Furthermore, Allie was the only black applicant for the position and the only opportunity for the black community to have a member of their race as superintendent.

SoJourner had gone to the paper because he felt black members were going to blame the white members for not including Allie in the second interview list, and he wanted the public to know the truth.

Porter Stewart and Freddie Williams criticized Dick for commenting on executive sessions, with Williams saying, "I think it is unethical."

The paper also carried a profile of the two finalists, both North Carolina superintendents. Both came from districts with lower SAT scores than Florence and with lower percentages of students taking the test.

Two days later at a budget study session, Porter Stewart, in a long, rambling statement, said board members need to honor the confidentiality of executive sessions. His statement did nothing to bring the board together.

The next day Dick SoJourner told me that Pat Evans called him after the meeting to propose a truce. According to Dick, Pat now supported Allie being a finalist. Glenn Odom also came by and expressed his support of Allie, but he said the black members would have to initiate any move to get Allie a second interview.

Two days later I walked into a budget study session to see Pat Evans, sitting at her seat at the horseshoe table, wearing a sandwich board that said, "I supported Allie Brooks." I'm sure she was disappointed that the press wasn't at the meeting.

The tension over the search for a superintendent spawned other problems for the board. At the close of the budget study session, James Littles accused former board members of trying to control the new board, referring to the former members as "ghosts." Littles then complained about the control of the agenda, saying current board members couldn't get their issues on the agenda.

When no one else responded to Littles, I did. "Any board member can put an item on the agenda. I covered this in the orientation meeting with you two days after you were elected. All you have to do is call me, and if you want an item on the agenda, it will be put there."

Littles thanked me, saying, "I'm glad you cleared that up." Pat Evans chimed in and said she didn't realize that board members could put items on the agenda.

Pat went on to say that she would not support fiscal independence until the board got its act together, referring to Dick SoJourner's breach of the confidentiality of the executive session over the superintendent finalists.

After the meeting Littles apologized to me, saying, "No offense, no offense."

The next day I listened to the tape of the orientation meeting. I had stated clearly that board members had a right to put items on the agenda. Additionally, I had given them an outline of my presentation, which included a section on how items get on the agenda. Each board member had a personal agenda and was not interested in teamwork.

Later on Wednesday, which was the day before the regular board meeting, Dick SoJourner came into my office and said, "I have an item for the agenda on Thursday." When I asked him what, he said, "Me." I repeated my question, and he repeated his answer. When I told him we needed a topic, he told me how tired he was of the behavior of black board members, especially the attacks on him.

I couldn't imagine going into a board meeting with "Dick SoJourner" as an agenda item. Dick's anger was affecting his judgment. Trying to get him to calm down, I suggested the topic be "Board Relationships," and he agreed.

Even though I could see "Board Relationships" as a legitimate topic for discussion, I didn't think Dick's approach would be helpful. I imagined the board meeting becoming a racial jihad. "Dick," I said, "this is a bad idea. Please don't do this."

The next day, when I got back from a meeting at 12:30, Dick was waiting on me.

"My sister-in-law just died, but I'm coming to the meeting tonight."

"The agenda is not long. You need to be with your family. You can miss the meeting. Everyone will understand."

"No, I want to be there. There's too many 5–4 votes," he said. He then showed me his statement and insisted that he wanted to be on the agenda.

The statement criticized the black members for their behavior and included comments about Freddie Williams's African dress. Unrepentant, Dick defended his going to the press over the Allie Brooks vote and said he would do it again if he felt the board was using executive sessions to cover inappropriate action.

I told him I thought his statement was a bad idea and asked him not to do it. He said he would think about it and call me. He called back in an hour and said he would not make his statement because I had asked him not to. He reiterated how tired he was of the behavior of the black members of the board. I thought we had dodged a disaster. I was wrong. The board meeting was the worst I ever attended, and once again, the problem was public participation.

Civil rights activist Freddie Jolley signed up for public participation, listing "suspensions, expulsions, staffing, and racism" as his topics. Porter Stewart decided to let Freddie go first.

Looking from side to side, surveying the board and the audience, Freddie approached the small table with a microphone. Taking the seat facing the board, Freddie told them he was not going to honor the five-minute time limit, challenging the board to call the police if they wanted to get him removed. Dodging the issue, Porter asked if he was speaking for a group. Freddie said no and proceeded.

As chair, Porter should have stopped Freddie at this point. When Porter let Freddie proceed, I looked at other board members, but they said nothing, looking down at the table in front of them, avoiding eye contact with anyone. Afraid the situation would escalate, no one did anything.

After complaining about the way a fight at South Florence High School was handled, saying we suspend and expel only black and poor students, and pleading a case for a parent who said her child couldn't get free juice and milk at school, Jolley demanded to know how many blacks were represented among the head coaches, assistant coaches, and athletic directors in the district. He then moved on to his primary reason for speaking to the board—Dick SoJourner.

Speaking directly to Dick, Jolley told him he could not criticize African American board members and tell them what to do. Porter tried to intervene and enforce the policy on personal attacks. Jolley wouldn't stop. He demanded SoJourner's resignation. Dick got up, said he was going to call the police, and left the room.

Jolley finished his attack and asked if board members had any questions. None did, and he went back to his seat in the audience.

The next speaker was the lady whose children could not get free milk at Wallace-Gregg Elementary School. She criticized Larry Leasure, the principal, saying he was never at the school, claiming the guidance counselor and the secretary ran the school. Porter did not try to stop her from this attack.

Since board meetings are open, protocol requires that the door to the meeting room be kept open. From my seat near the middle of the horseshoe table, I could see Dick SoJourner through the open door, pacing back and forth in the lobby, waiting for the police.

As an insurance agent was complaining about his child being suspended for having a beeper at school (a violation of state law), the police arrived. A young white police officer came to the door and beckoned for Freddie Jolley to come outside with him. Making sure everyone knew what was happening, Jolley said loudly, "Are you arresting me?"

Jolley got up and went outside. A couple of minutes later he stuck his head in the door and motioned for board member Freddie Williams to come outside. A couple of black men in the audience also went out with Williams.

The meeting continued, and eventually the people outside, including SoJourner and Jolley, came back. The policeman continued to wait in the lobby. Soon another officer joined him.

Before the meeting was over, Jolley left. When he did, Wade Jeffords, a reporter for the *Florence Morning News*, followed him outside. Wade came back, went outside, and came back again. None of the other spectators at the meeting seemed disturbed by the events, but I could sense everyone's relief when Jolley left the meeting. We continued with the board agenda.

Former board member Nancy Rawl followed the insurance agent in the public participation and asked the board to approve a special fund-raising project for South Florence.

As we were about to begin the business part of the meeting, a white lady with a lot of blonde hair, interrupted and asked to speak, saying she had contacted Glenn Odom about speaking at the meeting. Porter, in violation of our sign-up-in-advance rule, let her speak. She complained about the cost of field trips and about students being charged for assembly programs.

Finally we got to the agenda and ran through several routine items quickly. Porter then asked if the board wished to deal with Nancy Rawl's request. They added it to the agenda and approved the request.

We then moved into the discussion part of the agenda. The first item was the renewal of contracts. I had worried about board members having a lot of questions on this issue, but in the wake of the evening's excitement, it passed without comment.

Porter then called on me for a discussion of the budget. As I was talking, I noticed Elder James Williams in the audience raising his hand.

Doris Lockhart interrupted, saying to Porter that we had someone in the audience who wished to speak. Again, in violation of board rules, Porter let him speak.

. Williams was angry with the board for approving Nancy Rawl's request, pointing out that he had spoken to the board many times without a response at the meeting and sometimes not even after the meeting. He called the board's action "unconscionable" and vowed we would hear from him again. He got up and walked out of the meeting. Had he stayed a few minutes longer, he would have heard me recommend that the board pick up the salary of the Carver Community Center manager, whose advisory committee Williams chaired.

With Williams, Jolley, and several others gone from the meeting, I proceeded with my budget presentation. The board accepted my recommendations, and we had a budget for the coming year.

Next, I recommended that we advertise the two vacant assistant superintendent positions, wanting to begin the process so the new superintendent would be in a position to begin screening and interviewing immediately after his appointment. With Sara Slack and Gerald Holley both retiring, I felt their replacements needed to be hired as soon as possible to allow for a smooth transition.

Although no one said he or she didn't like the recommendation, it was clear the board wasn't going to accept it. I was thinking that we should advertise the positions so the new superintendent would have a pool of candidates to consider. I was not interested in getting involved in selecting assistant superintendents, but board members seemed to distrust my motives. They began questioning the necessity for advertising. It wasn't necessary, but it would have helped the new superintendent. Sensing their resistance, I dropped it.

We had planned to end the meeting with an eleven-minute video. The video had been developed by Pam McDaniel, the director of public information, in conjunction with South Carolina Educational Television. While the video was running, I told Porter how uncomfortable I was with what had happened at the meeting. He suggested we meet with Doris in my office after the meeting.

After the video, Porter was about to pronounce adjournment when Pat Evans interrupted. "If I'm not out of order, I'd like to make a motion that we invite Allie Brooks back into the pool of finalists for a second interview for the superintendent position." I thought she was out of order, but Porter didn't declare it so.

Glenn Odom spoke up immediately. "Since this is a personnel matter, we should discuss it in executive session."

Freddie Williams responded to Glenn. "Executive sessions are no good since Dr. SoJourner tells everything that goes on. If we go into executive session, I will leave."

Dick SoJourner seconded Pat's motion.

Joe Moyer said, "I'm not against Mr. Brooks, but I feel a decision has been made by the full board. Since Mr. Isgett is not here, taking a vote tonight would violate the selection process and make it void."

After Pat Evans and Doris Lockhart urged support of Pat's motion, Glenn Odom said, "I will be willing to discuss the matter in open session, but I cannot do so without commenting on what board members have said at previous executive sessions."

Glenn's comments complicated the issue for Pat Evans. She had opposed Allie in previous discussions and was supporting him now only because her constituents, in the aftermath of Dick SoJourner's leak to the newspaper, had become angry with her. She wanted now to publicly take a stand in favor of Allie, but she didn't want the previous discussions revealed in an open meeting.

Porter, picking up on Joe's comment, said he would entertain a motion to table and reschedule the meeting to discuss the matter when all board members could be present. Glenn made the motion to table; Joe Moyer seconded.

Pat Evans, thinking the motion had already been tabled, started complaining, not realizing a motion to table could not be debated, thinking her motion was not going to be discussed. I interrupted and told her the motion to table, which is a motion to postpone action, took priority and had to be voted on without debate.

A voice vote was inconclusive. On a show of hands, the motion passed 4–3 with Porter Stewart, Joe Moyer, Glenn Odom, and James Littles in favor of the motion to table. Porter asked Freddie Williams, who didn't vote, if he was abstaining. Williams replied, "No, I'm just not participating."

On my way to my office to meet with Porter and Doris, I passed Joe Moyer and Rick Reames. Joe said, "I wondered why you asked not to have your contract renewed. I understand now."

Rick said, "This is the third worst board meeting I've been in." I didn't want to hear about the other two.

Doris, Porter, and I met for about twenty minutes in my office. Angry that several people had ignored board rules and disrupted the meeting, I expressed my concern. "If an elected body, like this school board, can't hold a meeting without disruption, our society is not going to survive. Can you imagine the Congress of the United States allowing such disruption to the conduct of its business? We're at a smaller scale, but the board is an arm of the government and has a right to conduct its business according to its rules. We need a plan to deal with this type of disruption before the next meeting. If we're not going to enforce the rules we have, then we need to change our rules."

While Porter and Doris seemed to share my concern, their immediate priorities were to deal with Freddie Jolley and Elder James Williams, feeling we needed face-to-face follow-up meetings with them. We made no other plans, saying we would reflect on alternative courses of action and decide after sleeping on it.

It was 9:30 when I left for home and my evening meal.

The article in the Friday *Morning News* carried the headline, "Florence District 1 Defends Discipline, Hiring Practices." Wade Jeffords quoted South Florence High School principal Curt Boswell and me as saying both black and white students were suspended in the incident in which Freddie Jolley alleged only blacks were suspended.

On Saturday, March 14, the paper carried another story, "Tongue Lashing Gets Different Reactions." Pat Evans was quoted as saying, "I've never seen anything like it. I think it could have gotten out of hand if we hadn't handled it the way we did."

Doris Lockhart, unfazed by Jolley's behavior, said, "I know Mr. Jolley, and I've never seen him express his views any differently, so I wasn't afraid of anything getting out of hand. He could have been more tactful toward Mr. SoJourner."

When asked about his decision to call the police, Dick SoJourner said, "My experience with people who are, I call them psychotic, is that they don't let it die down. Porter Stewart should have done what I did."

When Doris, Porter, and I met with Freddie Jolley a few days later, I learned one reason for his attack. He was mad that Curt Boswell had suspended his son for throwing ice at a basketball game. Jolley said he only wanted fairness in hiring and disciplinary practices.

We didn't have a meeting of the minds with Elder Williams on the SFHS fund-raising project. He thought it was unfair for the board to approve the project. Williams then went on to one of his favorite topics—public participation at board meetings. Williams wanted the public to be able to participate more at board meetings, including participating in the discussion of items on the agenda. He asked that United for Students, the discipline advisory group on which he served, be empowered to recommend changes in the board's meeting rules and procedures.

The motion to give Allie Brooks a second interview was never taken off the table. Dick SoJourner talked with Allie, who said he didn't want to have anything to do with it. After that, it was never mentioned at a board meeting again.

Late in March the two superintendent finalists came to Florence for second interviews. Before the interviews, the public was invited to meet the candidates at a drop-in. Few people attended.

After David Bryant was announced as a finalist, board members and citizens from his community called board members in Florence to complain about him. In the process, Joe Nelson, superintendent of Bertie County, North Carolina, emerged as the favorite.

On April 16 the board met and approved a contract for Dr. Joe Nelson to become superintendent in the district. Dick SoJourner was miffed that the meeting was being held at 6:00 and threatened not to attend. When he realized the board was going to meet and act even if he was not there, he attended the session and agreed with the other eight board members to offer the position to Dr. Nelson.

After I asked the board not to renew my contract, I had begun looking for another job. With sixteen months to find another position, I thought I would leave long before the contract expired. I applied for several superintendencies and was not selected. The rejections hurt my pride and my confidence since most of the superintendencies were smaller and less prestigious than Florence. At fifty-seven, I felt old and used up.

I was offered an assistant superintendent's position in a South Carolina district, a position I would have enjoyed. But as the time neared when I would have to make a decision, I received an offer to become the executive director of the Pee Dee Education Center, a consortium of nineteen school districts in the Pee Dee region.

I was taking a cut of over $20,000 in pay, but I was a happy man. The Pee Dee Center's offices were just two blocks from the Florence One District offices so I would not have to bear the expense of relocating.

I accepted the position with the Pee Dee Education Center on May 14, 1998. That same night I met with the Florence School District One Board of Trustees for the last time. The meeting was horrible with bickering and arguing over minor matters, but I really didn't care. I was leaving.

I met with the board in executive session before the meeting and told them I would be leaving on May 29. I asked that they not make any comment on my leaving during the meeting. They honored my request. At 9:20 that night, I walked out of my last board meeting in Florence School District One.

Epilogue

The gulf between African Americans and whites in South Carolina is wide, deep, and growing. Dominated by two issues—the location of the Confederate flag on the Capitol grounds and the burnings of black churches—the 1990s were stressful times for racial relationships in the Palmetto State.

During the late 1990s, the South Carolina General Assembly devoted the lion's share of two sessions to the Confederate flag issue. In 1938 the battle flag of the Southern Confederacy had been placed behind the Speaker's desk in the South Carolina House of Representatives. In 1962 the General Assembly moved the flag to the top of the Capitol to fly beneath the U.S. and South Carolina flags.

African Americans never liked the Confederate flag flying over their state Capitol, and their resentment grew over the years. By the 1990s the state NAACP was determined to bring the flag down. The group called for an economic boycott of the state and staged a mass march to protest the flag's location.

Finally, in 2000, a compromise was reached, and the flag was moved from the Capitol dome to the Confederate memorial near Gervais Street. Although some African American leaders endorsed and supported the compromise, the NAACP rejected the new location and continued its boycott of the state.

During the 2004 session the General Assembly approved $380,000 a year for fifteen years to create the Palmetto Bowl to be played in Charleston. The assembly allocated these funds in spite of a National Collegiate Athletic Association moratorium against holding championship or postseason games in South Carolina as long as the Confederate flag is located on the statehouse grounds. The flag issue goes on and on.

Church burnings are another barometer of race relations in the state. Between October 1991 and June 10, 1996, twenty-seven black churches were burned in the state. In several instances members of the Ku Klux Klan were found culpable and punished for the crimes, but the rash of burnings across the state testified to the strain between the races in the Palmetto State.

The struggle to build Carver School in Florence took place in the context, and is a reflection of, the racial relationships in the state. The inability to work out problems between the races that characterizes much of South Carolina's history was a major factor in problems surrounding the construction of Carver School. African Americans and whites in Florence were able to talk to each other but were unable to empathize with the others' points of view. When leaders representing opposite points of view sat down to talk, no one was willing to compromise.

In communities where racial problems in schools have been resolved fairly and largely without rancor, leaders from both the African American and white communities have stepped forward and led the way. This didn't happen in Florence, where the community leaders were split, suspicious of each other, and bent on winning for their side.

Things are better now in Florence. Racial tensions in Florence School District One have eased since the change to single-member district representation for the school board.

In 2004 the Florence School District One Board of Trustees had five African Americans and four whites. Doris Lockhart served two years as chair of the board, the first African American woman to hold that position. Alexis Pipkins, another African American, followed Mrs. Lockhart as chair.

Controversy no longer clings to Carver School. Cynthia Young is still principal, and the school is integrated and enjoys a good reputation in the community.

No whites attend North Vista, but the district has moved REACH, the elementary gifted program, to that school. Each day approximately one hundred students, most of them white, attend the special program for the academically talented at North Vista.

As I left Florence School District One, I wondered how much students suffered from the amount of energy and resources devoted to controversial issues that diverted the focus from instruction.

In his first year as superintendent, Dr. Joe Nelson hired the Masonboro Group of Wilmington, North Carolina, to do an evaluation of the district's management and curriculum systems and to make recommendations for improvement. Dr. Eddie West, the lead consultant for the Masonboro Group, said his team was impressed with Florence School District One in terms of student performance and making the most of extremely limited resources.

West said, "The district typically performs near the top of the state on standardized tests and has an extremely low administrator-to-student ratio by state and national standards. Overall, the district is in terrific shape."

Since I had been Florence's superintendent for the previous eleven years, I read West's comments with great interest and satisfaction. With so much of my time and energy devoted to racial issues, I worried that I had neglected my main role, educating young people. The Masonboro audit relieved my anxieties about neglecting educational programs, but I knew we could have done a better job of educating the students in Florence One if we had not been so distracted by other issues.

In spite of the reduction in racial tension on the school board and between the board and community, I don't see signs that African Americans and whites are breaking down the barriers that have separated them over the years. Rather, I see blacks and whites in South Carolina like an old man and woman described in the poem, "Bar the Door."

The old couple has gone to bed when a gust of wind blows open the front door. Since it is cold outside and neither wants to get out of bed, they make a pact: the first one to speak has to get up and close the door.

Seeing the door open, a pair of robbers wanders into the couple's home. Since neither the man nor woman speak, the robbers make themselves at home, eating the couple's food and picking up personal belongings.

Recognizing that something strange is going on, the robbers decide to shave the old man's beard off and kiss the woman. The old man has had enough.

> O up then started out Goodman,
> An angry man wa he:
> "Will ye kiss my wife before my een,
> And scad me wi pudding-bree?"
> Then up and started our goodwife,
> Gied three steps on the floor:
> "Goodman, you've spoken the foremost word,
> Get up and bar the door."

In May 2004 the nation celebrated the fiftieth anniversary of the *Brown v. Board of Education* decision. You would think that fifty years would be sufficient time to complete the integration of schools, but you would be wrong. In fact, after three decades of progress, schools in South Carolina and the country are retreating from integration, and schools now are more segregated than they were in the mid-eighties.

Ironically, Florence School District One has bucked the trend and achieved a higher level of integration during the nineties. From 1990 to 2000, Florence School District One cut racial isolation by more than 50 percent as measured by the racial dissimilarity index. With 100 representing total segregation and 0 a perfectly integrated system, Florence School District One moved from an index of 50.3 in 1990 to 22 in 2000. Although controversial, the rezoning plan had worked to bring greater racial balance to the schools.*

Like Florence, most school districts now have met the legal requirements to integrate, but many communities are resegregating based on housing patterns. Additionally, in South Carolina and other states, conservative legislators push school choice and charter schools, devices that will further segregate students by race.

In July 2003 another historic trial began in Clarendon County, South Carolina, the birthplace of *Briggs v. Elliott.* Eight school districts sued the state for failure to provide a minimally adequate education. Eighty-eight percent of the students in these districts are minority members. More than 50 percent score below basic on the state accountability test.

Throughout the trial the state maintained it has provided an adequate education for these students, fighting the plaintiff districts in court. The trial lasted eighteen months, ending on December 9, 2004.

On October 5, 2005, after months of silence, Judge Thomas W. Cooper Jr. sent a letter to the attorneys, apologizing for the delay in issuing an opinion and committing to a decision by the end of the year. He kept his word. On December 29, 2005, Cooper issued his opinion, a 162-page document.

While both the state and the plaintiffs claimed to have won, neither side obtained a clear victory. Cooper ruled that the state is failing to provide students in the plaintiff districts with the opportunity for a minimally adequate education, but he limited the state's failure to an inadequate early childhood education program, saying the state must do more in this area. But Cooper did not specify actions for the state to take, nor did he impose a timetable for action.

The plaintiffs had sought relief for the funding of buildings and assistance in insuring that plaintiff districts were receiving quality teachers. The judge ruled that the state was meeting its obligation in these areas and required no further action by the state.

Cooper's ruling did little to resolve the issues raised in the case. In early 2006 the plaintiffs, undecided about an appeal, watched the General Assembly, looking for signs that the legislators would implement an improved early childhood education program. With the General Assembly limiting its discussion to expanding the state's program for four-year-olds, an appeal by the plaintiffs seems likely. The state has said it will not appeal unless the plaintiffs do.

---

* Data from Spatial Structures in the Social Sciences, "Desegregation Court Cases and School Desegregation Data," Brown University, http://www.s4.brown.edu/ schoolsegregation/schoolsegdatapage/codes/schoolseg.asp (accessed August 3, 2005).

South Carolinians continue to argue over who is going to "bar the door." But if South Carolina is to move forward as a state, then leaders from the white and African American communities must disentangle from the tentacles of the past, step forward and reach out to each other in good will, and find new ways of solving problems. Such leadership is critical in schools and school districts where the education of all children will be compromised by the time and energy wasted on clinging to the past.

Public schools have always faced challenges, but none greater than in the present time. Paul Houston, executive director of the American Association of School Administrators, commenting on the challenges facing superintendents and school board members, says we need men and women who have "enthusiasm for the impossible."

South Carolina's history suggests that racial harmony is impossible. After years of struggling with school integration, and with the apparent backsliding toward resegregating our society, it would be easy to give up on the dream of people of all races and creeds living in harmony and children of all colors receiving the kind of education that enables them to become effective citizens.

But if we learn from our past mistakes and embrace, with enthusiasm, the impossible dream of a better society for all, perhaps—just perhaps—schools will be truly integrated before we commemorate the hundredth anniversary of the *Brown* decision.

JANUARY 2006

Appendix

Florence School District One Board of Trustees

1992–93

Lawrence Orr, Chair
Anna Rose Rainwater, Vice-Chair
Randa Everett, Secretary
Miriam Baldwin
John Floyd Jr.
Mack Gettis
Glenn Odom
Dr. T. Carroll Player Jr.
Calvin Thomas

1993–94

Lawrence Orr, Chair
Anna Rose Rainwater, Vice-Chair
Randa Everett, Secretary
Miriam Baldwin
John Floyd Jr.
Doris Lockhart
Glenn Odom
Dr. T. Carroll Player Jr.
Calvin Thomas

1994–95

Anna Rose Rainwater, Chair
Glenn Odom, Vice-Chair
John Floyd Jr., Secretary
Miriam Baldwin
Randa Everett
Doris Lockhart
Lawrence Orr
Dr. T. Carroll Player Jr.
Dr. Richard H. SoJourner

1995–96

Anna Rose Rainwater, Chair
Glenn Odom, Vice-Chair
John Floyd Jr., Secretary
Miriam Baldwin
Doris Lockhart
Lawrence Orr
Dr. T. Carroll Player Jr.
Dr. Richard H. SoJourner
Porter Stewart

1996–97

Glenn Odom, Chair
John Floyd Jr., Vice-Chair
Porter Stewart, Secretary
Billy Isgett
Doris Lockhart
Dr. T. Carroll Player Jr.
Anna Rose Rainwater
Nancy Rawl
Dr. Richard H. SoJourner

1997–98

Porter Stewart, Chair
Doris Lockhart, Vice-Chair
Billy Isgett, Secretary
Patricia Evans
James Littles
Dr. Joe Moyer
Glenn Odom
Dr. Richard H. SoJourner
Freddie Williams

Index

Alexander, Terry, 61, 65, 102, 136
Allen, Dr. Josephine, 73
Alston, Dr. Clarence, 35, 55–57, 70–73,
    77, 88, 90, 111–13
Ames, Herbert, 65
Ames, Jane, 104
Ayers, Rick, 75

Bacote, Charles, 111–12
Baldwin, Miriam, 30, 38–39, 43–44, 59,
    68, 83–84, 93, 99, 125
Baptiste, Darnelle, 116
Barragan, Bruce, 116–21
Bartow School, 77
Beasley, Gov. David, 97
Bonds, Joe, 12
Boswell, Curt, 25, 47, 70, 94, 109, 151–52
Boulware, Harold, 2
Bowers, Bobby, 122–23, 129, 131
Briggs, Franklin, 100
Briggs Elementary School, 17, 23, 38, 87,
    98, 102, 126
Briggs v. Elliott, 2, 157
Brockington, Rosa, 42
Brooks, Allie, 70, 83, 144–47, 150–52
Brown, Rev. James, 68
Brown, Lionel, 35, 110
Brown v. Board of Education, 4, 156, 158
Bruce, Dr. John, 102

Bryant, David, 145, 152
Byrd, James, 13

Cain, Addie, 98
Carey, John, 115
Carey, Kelly, 46, 101
Carson, Joe, 25
Carter, Eleazor, 136, 141, 143
Carver Elementary School, 17, 38, 44, 89,
    115
Caulder, Trish, 116, 118, 120
Clarendon County, 3–4, 157
Clement Street, 41–46, 52–53, 62–63
Clemson University, 41–42, 44, 52
Clyburn, Congressman Jim, 97
Concerned Citizens for Excellence in
    Education, 59–60, 71, 74, 89
Cone, John, 19
controlled choice, 58–60
Cooper, Tommy, 70, 72, 97
Cribb, Debbie, 87
Crowley, Bruce, 10, 12–13
Cunningham, Leonye, 11, 44
Cunningham, Dr. Roy, 44–45, 99, 102,
    115–17, 119

Daise, Thad, 57
Danner, John, 12
Danville, Va., 19–21, 66, 100, 127

Davis, Lucy, 23, 30, 59, 102
Davis, Mary, 108
Davis, Patricia, 13
Delmae Elementary School, 66, 87,
    97–98, 100, 112
Dewey Carter Elementary School, 97
Dickey, Jerry, 106, 111–13
Diggs, Rev. W. P., 9, 11, 26–28, 42, 46,
    106
Dillon, Brynda, 137–38
Dixon, Sharon, 113
Dowdy, Natasha. 75
Duffy, Judge Michael, 101–2, 104

Edwards, Tommy, 35
Ellerbe, Dorothy, 17–18, 41, 54
Ervin, Teresa, 99, 102, 115–21
Evans, Pat, 137–40, 142, 145–47, 150–52
Everett, Randa, 30, 43–44, 67, 69, 80

Flood, Dr. Dudley, 45
Florence General Hospital, 19
Florence Morning News, 20, 34, 44, 61, 63,
    65, 67, 71, 86, 89, 91, 93, 96, 103–4,
    112, 122, 126, 133, 135, 137, 139,
    143–44, 149, 151
Florence School District One, 6–8, 11,
    19, 26, 28–30, 34, 45, 83, 92, 109,
    125–28, 143, 153
Floyd, John, 43–44, 46, 68, 71, 74, 77,
    80–84, 87, 101, 126–27, 129, 131–34,
    140
Fortier, Russ, 75
Foster, Dr. Gordon, 58–59
Fournier, Wayne, 97–98
Foxe, Charles, 68, 70–73, 99, 102, 112–13,
    116–17
Frate, Carolyn, 116–17
Frate, Dick, 23
Fulton, Catherine, 76

Gettis, Mack, 29
Gibbs, Mel, 117
Gilbert, Frank, 8, 12, 102, 108
Glover, Maggie, 13, 23, 25–26
Gordon, Dr. William, 83

Harmony Street, 62–63
Harrison, Alan, 36–37
Harrison, Jimmy, 89, 91, 102, 115–16
Hatton, Karen, 34
Hayes, Amy, 68
Henderson, Ellen, 134, 144
Henry, Sissy, 134, 144
Heyward, Evelyn, 33, 106–7
Heyward, Joe, 12–14
High, Belva, 12
Hill, Laurence, 10
Hodges, Gov. Jim, 5
Holley, Gerald, 46, 62, 123, 150
Hollings, Sen. Ernest, 97
Houston, Dr. Paul, 158
Huffman, Steffanie, 29, 34

International Baccalaureate (IB) program,
    69, 79–86
Isgett, Billy, 59, 65, 68, 71, 104, 119, 125,
    129–30, 132–34, 137, 140, 142, 145

Jackson, Bryan, 104
Jackson, Larry, 82, 97
Jeffords, Wade, 143, 145, 149, 151
Jolley, Freddie, 9–11, 13, 22, 138, 148–52
Jones, Glenn, 118–19
Jones, John, 11
Jordan, George, 10

Key Collins Firm, 41
Kinard, Tom, 104
King, Chris, 70–71, 73
Koon, Randy, 72

Lamar Bus incident, 6–7
Leasure, Larry, 148
Leatherman, Sen. Hugh, 38
Leatherman, Jean, 38, 59
Lester, Theodore, 7–8, 10, 131
Lester Elementary School, 33–34, 105–6,
    109
Littles, James, 137–38, 141–47, 151
Lockhart, Doris, 43–45, 50, 56, 61–62,
    64, 67, 69, 77, 80–81, 83, 85, 91, 93,
    96, 101, 106–7, 118–20, 130–32,

134–35, 137–38, 140–42, 145–46,
149–50, 152, 155
Lott, Hamilton, 53
Lucas, David, 13, 28

Magee, Pat, 94, 96
Marschel, Tom, 93
Marshall, Thurgood, 2
Mashack, Rev. Willie, 120
Maurer, Michael, 46, 62, 69–70, 81–86,
88–89, 93, 100–101, 103
McAllister, Rev. Julius, 39–40
McAllister, William, 59, 68, 70–72, 76
McClenaghan High School, 4, 7
McCutcheon, Rev. Larry, 39, 42–43, 63,
70–75, 91, 106, 117–18
McFadden, Helen, 129
McIntosh, Laurence, 6–7, 11, 22–23, 46,
52–53, 63, 65, 69, 81–83, 85–89, 93,
100–3, 106, 109, 122–23, 128–32,
135–36, 141–43
McLaurin Elementary School, 87, 98
McMakin, Rita, 38, 40
Mechanicsville Road, 44, 46
Miley, Jane, 123
Moore Intermediate School, 67, 87, 113
Morning News. See *Florence Morning News*
Moyer, Dr. Joe, 59, 68, 137, 142, 150–51

NAACP, 4, 5, 10–11, 13, 27–28, 42–43,
45–46, 51–53, 62–63, 66, 70, 89, 92,
100, 103, 122–23, 125, 128–29, 131–32,
135–37, 141–43, 154
Nelson, Dr. Joe, 152, 155
Newkirk, Bill, 36–37
News Journal, 63
North Vista Education Committee
(NVEC), 68, 70–78, 89–90, 102
North Vista Elementary School, 35, 43,
55, 57, 60–62, 66–78, 80–81, 83–86,
88–90, 93, 96, 100–3, 111–14, 155
Northwest Community Council, 45, 89,
91–92, 95, 102, 115–17, 119, 121

Odom, Glenn, 43–44, 50–51, 59–61, 68,
80, 83–85, 87, 93, 109, 126, 128, 132,

134–35, 138, 140–42, 145–46, 149–51
Orangeburg Massacre, 5
Orr, Larry, 25, 30, 42–44, 49, 69, 77, 84,
88, 101, 103, 109, 125

Pate, David, 30
Pearson, Levi, 3
Pee Dee Education Center, 153
Pee Dee Times, 44–45, 75, 116–17
Pierce, Eugene, 11
Player, Dr. Carroll, 23, 25, 29–31, 43–44,
50–51, 69, 76–77, 80–81, 83–86, 88, 93,
101, 126, 129–32, 140
Porter, Ralph, 35–36
Poston, Judith, 96
Poynor Adult Center, 50, 52–53, 58, 67,
74, 100, 115, 117
Price, Dr. Julian, 7, 131
Pridgen, Denise, 61–62, 71, 86, 89–90
Pringle, Melinda Graham, 75
Proffitt, Dr. Brank, 121

Rainwater, Anna Rose, 30, 42, 44, 50–53,
56, 61, 63, 65–66, 69, 74, 76, 78,
80–85, 87, 91, 93–102, 104, 107, 109,
130, 132, 134
Rawl, Nancy, 59, 65, 70, 74, 102, 125,
129, 134, 137–38
REACH (Reaching Exceptionally Able
Children), 85
Reames, Rick, 58–60, 89, 91, 97, 100–2,
111–12, 136, 151
Reddix-Smalls, Brenda, 53, 122, 130–31
Reid, Dr. Isaiah, 72–78, 83–85
Revell, Jo Anne, 133
Robinson, Ed, 65, 92, 106
Robinson, Madie, 13
Ross, Robert, 36
Royall Elementary School, 17, 38, 87, 97,
102–3
Russell, Judge Donald, 7

Sanford, Gov. Mark, 5
Savannah Grove Elementary School, 17,
35, 38, 97, 110
Sayle, Frank, 93

School Safety Committee, 50

Scott, Nancy, 74

Seymore, Judge Margaret, 129, 131–32

Shaw, Paul, 145

Slack, Sara, 33, 57, 71, 91, 110, 150

Smith, Harriet, 99, 115–16, 118–20

Smith, Julie, 70, 73

Smith, June, 102

Smith, Martin, 98–99, 126–27

Smith, Rebecca, 98

Smith, Dr. Seth, 59–61, 68, 70–72

Sneed, Henry, 5, 54

SoJourner, Dr. Richard, 51, 61, 63, 67–68, 74, 76–77, 80–81, 83, 85, 88, 93, 112, 126–27, 129–30, 132, 134, 137, 141–43, 145–52

South Carolina School Boards Association, 13, 19, 134, 144

South Florence High School, 13, 25–27, 47–48, 68, 94, 108–9, 139, 148–9

Southside Middle School, 20, 22–23, 49, 96

Stewart, Porter, 87, 120, 122, 130, 134, 137–38, 140, 142, 145–46, 148–52

Stoddard, Dan, 126

Stokes Road, 42–43

Sullivan, Jack, 13

Sumter/Cashua, 62–64, 90

Swartz, Donna, 123

Thomas, Calvin, 10, 13, 20, 23–24, 26–32, 34–35, 43–46, 49–51, 53, 62–63, 91–93, 103–4, 106, 109, 128, 135–37, 143

Thurmond, Sen. Strom, 7, 97

Tisdale, Jane, 123

Traxler, Judge William, 122–23, 129, 131–32, 141–43

Truitt, Judy, 19–20

U.S. Department of Justice, 7, 45–46, 51, 53, 57, 59, 61–62, 65–69, 72, 74–75, 79–82, 85, 88, 90, 92–93, 97, 100–2, 105, 113, 123, 125

Wallace, Mike, 68, 74–75

Weldon, Weston, 23, 27

Wells, Lisa, 38, 40

West, Dr. Eddie, 155

West Florence High School, 13–14, 29, 35–37, 48, 66, 79, 99

Wilkes, Jerry, 22, 34, 53, 94, 136

Williams, Freddie, 137–43, 145–47, 149–51

Williams, Elder James, 59, 61, 67–68, 70, 72–73, 75, 92, 94–99, 102, 106, 112–13, 149–52

Williams, Marlene, 105–6, 109

Williams Middle School, 12, 23, 69, 79–86, 93, 97

Willis, Mayor Frank, 115

Wilson High School, 8–10, 13, 49, 66, 69, 79–81, 83–86, 93, 99, 113, 144–45

Womack, Jim, 13–14, 24

Woodard, Rick, 59

Wukela, Steve, 106–10

Yeatts, Guy, 66

Young, Cynthia, 54, 91–92, 155

About the Author

THOMAS E. TRUITT's career in education has spanned forty-three years and three states. As a teacher, principal, assistant superintendent, and superintendent, he helped to integrate schools in Burlington, North Carolina, and Danville, Virginia. In South Carolina he served as Florence District One superintendent for eleven years and as executive director of the Pee Dee Education Center, a consortium of nineteen school districts in South Carolina. Truitt holds an Ed.D. in school administration from the University of North Carolina at Chapel Hill. He lives in Columbia, South Carolina.